KINGFISHER KNOWLEDGE

WONDERS OF THE WORLD

▶ Japan's Akashi-Kaikyo Suspension Bridge opened in 1998,
linking the city of Kobe to Awaji island. It has a total length of
almost 2.5 mi. (4km) and is designed to withstand winds as high as
177 mph (285km/h) and earthquakes of up to 8.5 on the Richter scale.

WONDERS OF THE WORLD

Philip Steele

Foreword by

Françoise Rivière

**Assistant Director-General for Culture, UNESCO
(United Nations Educational, Scientific,
and Cultural Organization)**

KINGFISHER
BOSTON

Editors: Vicky Bywater, Miranda Smith,
  Hannah Wilson
Coordinating editor: Caitlin Doyle
Designers: Malcolm Parchment, Rebecca Painter
Consultant: Dr. Miles Russell, School of Conservation
  Studies, Bournemouth University, U.K.
Picture research manager: Cee Weston-Baker
Senior production controller: Teresa Wood
DTP manager: Nicky Studdart
DTP operator: Claire Cessford
Proofreader: Ronne Randall

GO FURTHER . . .
INFORMATION PANEL KEY:

web sites and
further reading

career paths

places to visit

KINGFISHER

a Houghton Mifflin Company imprint
222 Berkeley Street
Boston, Massachusetts 02116
www.houghtonmifflinbooks.com

First published in 2007
10 9 8 7 6 5 4 3 2 1
1TR/0107/TWP/MA(MA)/130ENSOMA/F

ISBN 978-0-7534-5979-9

Copyright © Kingfisher Publications Plc 2007

LIBRARY OF CONGRESS CATALOGING-IN-PUBLICATION DATA
Wonders of the world / Philip Steele.—1st ed.
    p. cm.—(Kingfisher knowledge)
    Includes bibliographical references and index.
    1. Civilization, Ancient—Juvenile literature. 2.
Civilization, Modern—Juvenile literature. 3. Curiosities
and wonders—Juvenile literature. 4. Historic
buildings—Juvenile literature. 5. Historic sites—
Juvenile literature. 6. Antiquities—Juvenile literature.
7. Architecture—Juvenile literature. 8. Seven Wonders
of the World—Juvenile literature. I. Title.
    CB151.S76 2007
    930.1—dc22   2006022516

Printed in Singapore

Contents

Foreword   6

CHAPTER 1
SEVEN ANCIENT
WONDERS   7

The Great Pyramid   8–9
Marvels of Babylon   10–11
Olympic Zeus   12–13
Temple of the Goddess   14–15
The Mausoleum   16–17
The Colossus of Rhodes   18–19
Pharos of Alexandria   20–21
Summary   22

▼ The Great Pyramid in Giza, Egypt, is the only
survivor of the seven wonders of the ancient world.

CHAPTER 2
THE WIDER WORLD   23

Colosseum in Rome	24–25
Great Wall of China	26–27
Angkor Wat	28–29
Pacific Ocean mysteries	30–31
Chichén Itzá	32–33
The Taj Mahal	34–35
Canals of Venice	36–37
Summary	38

CHAPTER 3
MODERN WONDERS   39

On top of the world!	40–41
Architecture and the arts	42–43
Water wonders	44–45

Building bridges	46–47
Info lab	48–49
Modern colossi	50–51
Reaching other worlds	52–53
Summary	54

World heritage	55–59
Glossary	60–61
Index	62–63
Acknowledgments	64

NOTE TO READERS

Foreword

In ancient times there were seven wonders of the world. These were places that were so beautiful, so unique, that they were considered to be the most extraordinary places in the world. Nowadays, only one of these places is left: the pyramids in Egypt, with the famous sphinx. This is now a World Heritage Site.

In 1972 UNESCO adopted the convention concerning the Protection of the World Cultural and Natural Heritage. This is an agreement signed by 182 countries in the world. Each country that signs this agreement makes a promise to protect their own heritage—but also to help other countries protect theirs. To date, 812 sites have been recognized as places so important for the whole of humanity that they deserve to be protected by the international community as a whole.

There are many wonderful places around the world. Some of them are incredible achievements of human imagination and skills—for example, the Eiffel Tower in my home country of France. In Tsodilo, Botswana ancient rock-art drawings show us how people first used to communicate through art, and there are fantastic modern buildings such as Antoni Gaudi's works in Barcelona, Spain. This book looks at many of the wonders that have been built by people throughout the ages. There are also extraordinary natural places, from the brightly colored corals of Australia's Great Barrier Reef to the tropical rain forests of Sumatra, Indonesia, or the huge plains of the Serengeti in Tanzania. Sometimes these are only home to certain animal and plant species, so it is essential that we keep them safe as well.

If we do not take care of these magnificent places, they will disappear. That is why it is important for all of us to know about them and find out how to protect them.

What is the heritage of your own country? You may know about sites like Stonehenge—the stone circles in England where Druids used to meet—or the amazing pyramids in Egypt. Do you know that similar stone circles are World Heritage Sites in Senegal and Gambia, and that the earliest human fossil site is located in South Africa?

You can learn about the heritage that is near you, and you can visit and see for yourself. With the help of this book and the links that it provides, you can also find out about places that are important to peoples of other countries. The better we know a place, the better we will care for it in the future.

Françoise Rivière
Assistant Director-General for Culture, UNESCO
(United Nations Educational, Scientific, and Cultural Organization)

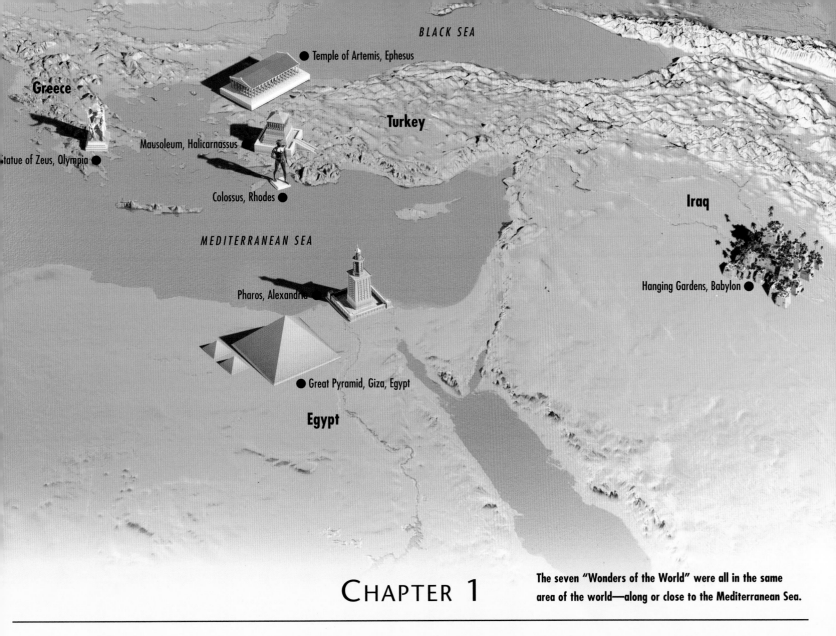

BLACK SEA

● Temple of Artemis, Ephesus

Greece

Turkey

Mausoleum, Halicarnassus

Statue of Zeus, Olympia ●

Colossus, Rhodes ●

Iraq

MEDITERRANEAN SEA

Pharos, Alexandria

Hanging Gardens, Babylon ●

● Great Pyramid, Giza, Egypt

Egypt

CHAPTER 1

The seven "Wonders of the World" were all in the same area of the world—along or close to the Mediterranean Sea.

Seven ancient wonders

Tourism is nothing new. More than 2,000 years ago Greeks and Romans were traveling to faraway lands, including Egypt, to see the sights. They visited monuments such as the Great Pyramid of Khufu, which then was more than 2,500 years old. Travelers boasted about their voyages, telling tales of the amazing things that they had seen. The Greek writers Herodotus (484–420 B.C.) and Callimachus of Cyrene (305–240 B.C.) wrote lists of these wonders. A poet named Antipater of Sidon, who was writing in around 120 B.C., made a chart of the top seven attractions. Through the Roman period and the Middle Ages, writers became fascinated with the "Seven Wonders of the World," and those of the ancient world are now established. But the idea of choosing wonders is something that is still popular to this day.

The Great Pyramid

Today three massive stone monuments tower over the desert in Giza, close to the modern-day Egyptian city of Cairo. The largest of these monuments is the Great Pyramid, which was sited between the Nile river and the Western Desert and built over a 20-year period, finishing around 2560 B.C. It contains the burial chamber of Khufu, an Egyptian pharaoh who died in 2566 B.C. Today visitors to the Great Pyramid are still struck with awe. Imagine how it must have looked when it was first built, covered in shimmering white limestone and topped with gold.

▲ Close to the Great Pyramid is a statue with the body of a lion and the head of a man. Its face probably represents the pharaoh Khafra, who died in 2532 B.C. This mysterious monument has fascinated people for more than 4,500 years.

Built on a gigantic scale

A true pyramid has a square base, from which four flat sides converge to a point. The Great Pyramid was originally 479 ft. (146m) high—it is shorter today because the stone at the top is missing—and the base measured 754 ft. (230m) from corner to corner. The word "pyramid" is Greek, not Egyptian, and it is named after a small wheat cake that the Greeks used to bake, which was a similar shape. It hardly seems a suitable word for such a massive structure. This pyramid was made up of more than two million stone blocks, each one averaging 2.5 tons in weight.

◄ The Great Pyramid was surrounded by temples and smaller pyramids. Later two other great tombs were added to the temple complex, the pyramids of Khafra and Menkaura.

▲ The earliest type of pyramid in Egypt had stepped sides. This was the tomb of the pharaoh Djoser in Saqqara. He died in 2648 B.C. The core of the Great Pyramid was also stepped, but it was finished by filling in the steps and covering the surface with limestone to make smooth, flat sides.

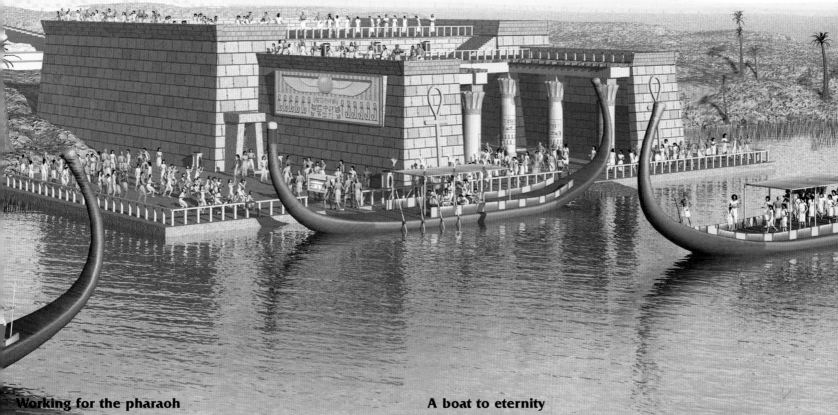

Working for the pharaoh

Giza must have been one of the biggest construction sites in history, bustling with architects, stonemasons, surveyors, and several thousand workers. All sweated under a blazing sun. The man-made mountain may have taken up to 20 years to complete, and there were also temples and riverside piers to build. The work was not carried out by slaves but by thousands of ordinary citizens. They were expected to offer their services to the state each year when floods on the Nile river forced them to stop farming for a few months.

A boat to eternity

When Khufu died, his body was carried by boat across the Nile river to the temples in Giza and then sealed inside one of three burial chambers in the Great Pyramid. The Egyptians believed that the survival of their whole world depended on the pharaoh traveling successfully to the afterlife—the pyramid was, in effect, a giant launching pad for the spirit of the dead ruler. In fact, Khufu did gain a kind of immortality, since his tomb ensured that his name would live on. For thousands of years the Great Pyramid remained the world's largest and most famous building.

Marvels of Babylon

Babylon was one of the world's first great cities. It was in the heart of Mesopotamia, a region of western Asia that covered a similar area to modern-day Iraq. Babylon is often mentioned in ancient Greek lists of the seven wonders. Most writers praised the legendary "Hanging Gardens" of Babylon, but others were more impressed with Babylon's massive city walls.

◀ It was said that the ruler Nebuchadnezzar II built the Hanging Gardens for his wife Amytis. She was from the green mountains of the northeast and was unhappy with the dusty plains around Babylon. They both loved to wander along the lush terraces of the gardens.

Cradle of civilization

Mesopotamia has been called the "cradle of civilization." It was there that the first towns and cities in history were built, laws were first written, and the world's first empires were created. Mesopotamians invented writing, the 60-minute hour, and the wheel. Babylon, already a city of around 200,000 people, became the center of a great empire in the 1900s B.C. It had another great period of power after 625 B.C., and it was this second empire that was admired and talked about by Greek travelers.

▶ The word "paradise" originally meant a walled garden. Gardens were highly valued in ancient Mesopotamia and Persia and were laid out around many royal palaces. In a hot, dry land sprinkling fountains and shaded pools seemed to be the ultimate luxury. As the Babylonian Empire grew larger, all types of palm trees, exotic shrubs, luscious fruits, and fragrant flowers might have been brought back to be planted in Babylon's Hanging Gardens.

The age of Nebuchadnezzar II

Babylon was built beside the Euphrates river, which provided precious water in a dry region. A sacred monument towered over the city—a huge ziggurat, or stepped pyramid. Babylon was also the center of trade, jewelry-making, weaving, astronomy, mathematics, and learning. The city was rebuilt by the powerful king Nebuchadnezzar II, who reigned from 605 to 562 B.C. The outer wall of his new city was 11 mi. (18km) long and 79 ft. (24m) thick. Its gates were glazed in blue and decorated with mythical creatures. A war chariot could turn around on top of the wall—and that alone made it a wonder of the world for some Greeks.

The Hanging Gardens

The Greek word *kremastos* actually means either "hanging" or "overhanging," and it is likely that the gardens on the terraces "overhung" the city. But were the terraces of the city really planted with exotic trees, vines, and flowering shrubs? Some archaeologists claim to have found traces of the gardens, but others do not believe that they existed in the first place. The gardens are not mentioned in Babylonian records. Were the Greeks thinking of the palace gardens in Nineveh instead? We may never know.

▲ Greek descriptions of the Hanging Gardens mention concealed channels of water designed to keep the roots of the plants moist. The water wheel feeding buckets above may have been the type of device that was used to push water through the concealed channels. Mesopotamian civilization depended on irrigation, building canals, and water engineering. It was these skills, developed in the region over a period of thousands of years, that were so admired by the Greeks.

Olympic Zeus

Zeus was the king of the Greek gods and the lord of the sky. He was the bringer of justice, who hurled thunderbolts at wicked humans. In around 430 B.C. the Greeks erected a magnificent statue to Zeus that showed him in all of his majesty and power. The statue was created by Phidias, the greatest of all Greek sculptors. It was placed in a temple at the sacred site of Olympia in southwestern Greece, which was the home of the famous ancient religious and sporting festival—the Olympic Games.

▶ This statue of Zeus stood in a temple that had been built in 457 B.C. The figure of the god was around 40 ft. (12m) high and carved out of ivory. His robes were made of gold. In one hand he held a life-size statue of Nike, the goddess of victory; in the other hand he held a scepter topped with a golden eagle.

◀ The ruins of the temple of Zeus can still be visited today. Olympia had been a sacred site for a long time, and the goddess Hera was also worshiped there. Beneath the blue skies and the hot sunshine the dark groves of trees offered shade and peace.

The Olympic Games

Olympia was never a town in its own right, although it offered accommodation and places for visitors to eat. Travelers came to Olympia because of its famous games, which started in 776 B.C., or even earlier. The games were a festival of athletic skills. They had begun with just running events and wrestling bouts, but eventually they also included horse races, chariot races, boxing, and racing in armor. Competitors came from all over Greece and from distant Greek settlements overseas. Successful athletes were celebrated and became very famous.

▼ On the front of the temple of Zeus statues showed scenes from Greek mythology. Below an ancient tribe called the Lapiths are battling with the centaurs, who are half-human and half-horse.

Honoring the gods

The Olympic Games were held every four years. They were an important occasion to show off physical prowess, and included great feasting and drinking. Only men could attend, although there were separate female games that were held in honor of the goddess Hera. Around 40,000 spectators could fit into the stadium. However, the Olympic Games were more than just a sports contest. They were also a deeply religious occasion and were primarily a religious festival held to honor Zeus, the father of the Greek gods and goddesses. None of the Greek states could go to war during the Olympic Games, and sacrifices were made to the gods. It was only fitting that the king of the gods would be honored there.

▶ Throwing sports at the ancient Olympic Games included the discus (right) and the javelin. This lifelike statue of a discus thrower in action dates from around 460 B.C. Discus throwing is still an Olympic sport today.

▼ More than 11,000 athletes from 202 countries competed in the 2004 Olympic Games, held in Athens, Greece. The spectacular closing ceremony in the main stadium was watched by around 70,000 spectators.

An end and a new beginning

The statue of Zeus in Olympia was hailed as one of the wonders of the ancient world. However, hundreds of years later, when the Greeks became Christians, the old gods were looked down on. Emperor Theodosius I banned the Olympic Games in A.D. 393. By this time, the statue of Zeus had been carried off to the newly built Greek city of Constantinople (modern-day Istanbul). Sadly, the statue of Zeus was destroyed there by a fire in A.D. 462. However, the story does have a happy ending. The Olympic Games were eventually revived in 1896, and they are now the most important athletic contest in the world and are held in a different country every four years.

Temple of the goddess

Foreign kings, merchants, pilgrims, and travelers came from far distances to see the Artemisium—the great temple in Ephesus (in present-day Turkey). They left gold, silver, and jewelry there as offerings to the goddess Artemis. Visitors were awestruck by this incredible building, which seemed to reach up to the clouds. Ancient writers reported that the temple was more impressive than the pyramids in Egypt or the city of Babylon. Some hailed it as the greatest wonder of the world.

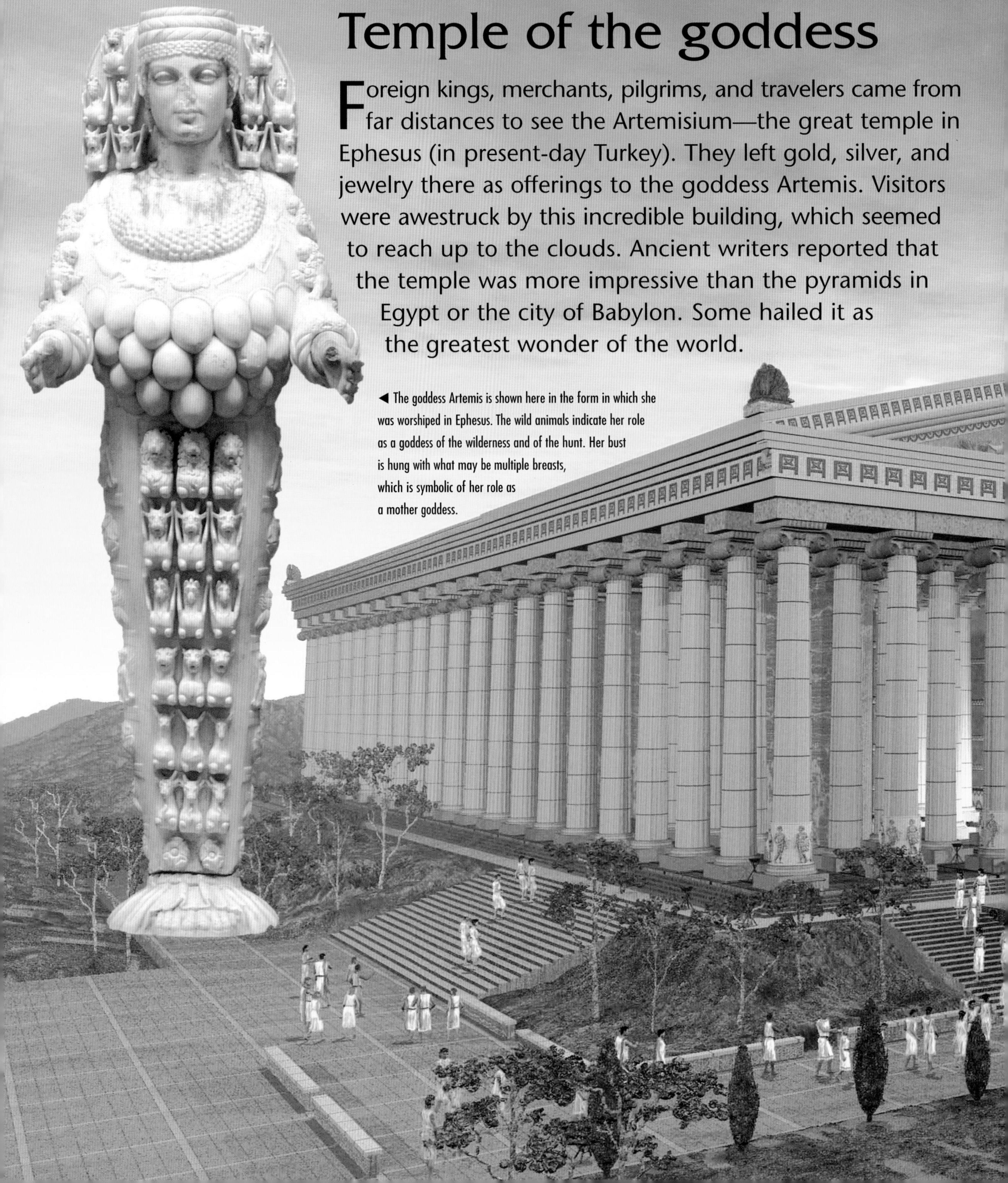

◄ The goddess Artemis is shown here in the form in which she was worshiped in Ephesus. The wild animals indicate her role as a goddess of the wilderness and of the hunt. Her bust is hung with what may be multiple breasts, which is symbolic of her role as a mother goddess.

A city by the sea

Today the eastern coast of the Aegean Sea is part of Turkey. In ancient times it was the home of various peoples of the region. The Greeks settled there in around 1050 B.C. and built a city in Ephesus. This reached the height of its wealth in the 500s B.C. For a while, Ephesus was under the rule of the Persian Empire. Even before the Greeks arrived, the site of Ephesus had been sacred to a mother goddess named Cybele. The way in which Cybele was worshiped soon became mixed up with the ceremonies that were carried out for a Greek goddess named Artemis, and the Greeks built temples in her honor.

The goddess

Work on a new temple dedicated to Artemis was started in Ephesus in around 550 B.C., and the building was completed around 120 years later. In Greek mythology Artemis was worshiped as the twin sister of the sun god, Apollo, and was known as the "lady of wild animals." She was also the goddess of wild places. Artemis was often shown hunting with a bow and arrows. In Ephesus she was represented more often as a goddess of fertility and childbirth. The Roman name for Artemis was Diana.

Marble and fire

The base of the temple in Ephesus was 377 ft. (115m) long and 180 ft. (55m) wide. It was built out of gleaming white marble, and its 127 columns were 59 ft. (18m) high. In 356 B.C. the Artemisium was burned down by a young man named Herostratus, who thought that this act would make him famous forever. The temple was rebuilt in around 250 B.C., but it was destroyed again by the Goths—northern European warriors who raided Ephesus in A.D. 262. The last remains of the temple were torn down by Christians at the beginning of the A.D. 400s. The site was not rediscovered until 1869.

▼ In ancient times the temple site was busy with traders selling items to pilgrims. On festival days there would be sacrifices of bulls at the altar. Religious processions followed a sacred route that led from the town to the temple of Artemis.

▶ The bases of the temple's columns were made out of marble, and some displayed beautiful carvings. Like most of the stonework, they would have originally been painted with bright colors. Other parts of the Artemisium were adorned with colorful paintings.

The Mausoleum

In the 300s B.C. travelers sailing along the eastern coast of the Aegean Sea brought back tales of an awesome building. It was the tomb of a ruler named Mausolus and stood in the city of Halicarnassus. This memorial to Mausolus was called the Mausoleum, and it became so famous that, today, any tomb that is designed as a grand public monument also uses the name "mausoleum."

▶ Mausolus was a native of Caria. He governed the region at a time when it was part of the Persian Empire. However, he rebelled against the rulers of the day and managed to win personal control of Caria and the neighboring territories.

The life of Mausolus

Halicarnassus stood on the site of the modern-day town of Bodrum, in Turkey. The region, known as Caria, was home to the Greeks and other Aegean peoples. According to the royal custom in those days, Mausolus married his sister, Artemisia. Together, they created an impressive new capital city in the Greek style in Halicarnassus.

Mausolus and Artemisia started building the most magnificent tomb that the world had ever known. When Mausolus died in 353 B.C., it was up to Artemisia to make sure that the project was completed as planned.

Artemisia's creation

As soon as they heard of her brother's death, the islanders of Rhodes rose up against Artemisia, but she crushed their rebellion. Then she made sure that only the best Greek architects, builders, sculptors, and craftsmen were employed to finish the tomb. It was located on a hill above the town and was completed in 350 B.C. Artemisia died soon afterward. Her ashes were placed in the Mausoleum alongside those of her brother.

The perfect monument

The Mausoleum was set on a massive tiered platform adorned with stone lions and statues of gods and warriors. The marble tomb was decorated with images from Greek mythology, including centaurs (half-human and half-horse) and Amazons (female warriors). There were soaring columns and a massive roof that was topped with a gleaming chariot made of gold drawn by four horses. The tomb survived until the Middle Ages, but it was then wrecked by a series of earthquakes. Rescued by archaeologists, parts of the tomb can still be seen today in the British Museum in London, England.

◄ The Mausoleum above the town was around 148 ft. (45m) high and had 36 columns, nine on each side, set around a central block that supported the stepped roof. The base measured around 130 ft. by 98 ft. (40m by 30m). This beautiful memorial was part of an ambitious building scheme in Halicarnassus, which included a citadel, dockyards, city walls, and many other monuments and statues.

▲ What impressed visitors to the Mausoleum most was the lifelike quality of its many statues and friezes. The stone-carved scene above shows a fierce battle between Greek warriors and Amazons, the warlike female race described in ancient Greek poems such as Homer's *Iliad*.

The Colossus of Rhodes

Sailors would gaze upward in awe as their sailing boats entered the ancient harbor of the Greek island of Rhodes. Towering above them was a gigantic statue of Helios, the sun god. As the sailors squinted against the dazzling sunlight reflected off the statue's bronze casing, they could see a crown of rays shimmering against the blue sky. The statue stood on a 49-ft. (15-m)-high marble base and was an amazing 112 ft. (34m) tall.

▶ The Colossus was built by the sea so that all visitors to Rhodes would be impressed. It was later said to straddle the harbor entrance, with ships passing between its legs. In reality, it was probably built to the east of the harbor. Swords and spears that had been abandoned by Demetrius's army were melted down and used in this new monument to peace. Abandoned siege towers were built into the scaffolding. The core of the structure was made out of stone blocks reinforced with iron. The outer skin of the statue was made from plates of bronze.

War and peace

The story of the "Colossus," the giant statue of Rhodes, began with a war. The islanders of Rhodes had made an alliance with the Greek ruler of Egypt, Ptolemy I. Another powerful ruler, Antigonus I of Cyprus, tried to put an end to this alliance by sending his son Demetrius to besiege Rhodes. In 304 B.C. Demetrius was forced from the island, and the islanders began their victory celebrations. They decided to ask the sculptor Chares of Lindos to commemorate the peace by building a giant statue of the island's most important god, Helios. Construction took place between 292 and 280 B.C.

The fall of Helios

Few travelers could ever forget Rhodes and its giant bronze statue. The torch in its hand could even be lit to be used as a beacon to guide ships. Everyone agreed that the Colossus was a wonder of the world. Sadly, it was toppled by an earthquake in around 226 B.C. and lay on the ground in ruins for almost 1,000 years. The islanders refused to rebuild the statue because they believed that they had offended Helios in some way and that he had caused the statue to fall. The remains of the Colossus are said to have been eventually sold and the bronze pieces carried to Syria on the backs of 900 camels.

◀ A coin portrays Helios, the god of the sun, with his crown of rays. Helios was believed to drive his fiery chariot acros the sky during the day, before sinking under the waves at sunset. A festival of Helios was held on the island, during which a chariot with four horses was driven over a cliff into the sea to symbolize the setting of the sun. The god was especially honored on Rhodes, a tradition that may have come to the island from the Asian mainland, which lies just 10 mi. (16km) to the east. It was said that the people of Rhodes were descended from the god's seven sons.

Pharos of Alexandria

Of all the wonders of the ancient world, only one served a practical purpose. This was the Pharos, a tall lighthouse that guarded the harbor in Alexandria, Egypt. The city of Alexandria had been founded by the Greek leader Alexander the Great in 331 B.C. One of the generals who fought with him became the Greek ruler of Egypt in 323 B.C., taking the title of Ptolemy I. Ptolemy ordered work to begin on this building project in around 290 B.C. The tower was completed during the reign of his son, Ptolemy II.

▲ Ptolemy II, known as Philadelphus, was the ruler of Egypt when the Pharos of Alexandria was finished. His father, Ptolemy I, had begun the project around 20 years before.

▶ Today Pharos island in Alexandria is occupied by a citadel, which forms part of the coastal defenses that were built in A.D. 1480 by the Egyptian sultan Al-Ashraf Qaitbay. Some of the larger stones used in its construction came from the original Pharos.

A landmark for sailors

For sailors traveling to Alexandria from Greece, the Egyptian coastline appears low on the horizon and often shimmers in a heat haze. Ptolemy I decided that sailors needed a navigation aid to mark the entrance to the harbor. He ordered the architect Sostratus of Cnidus to build a high tower on a small, rocky island called Pharos, which was connected to the mainland by a sea wall. Soon the whole tower became known as "the Pharos." After the Romans began to rule Egypt in 30 B.C., the tower was transformed into the world's most famous lighthouse. The signal could be given out either be a dazzling mirror that reflected the rays of the sun or by a blazing beacon that was visible at night.

The tower tumbles

The Pharos was more than 295 ft. (90m) high, and it was claimed that seafarers could see the light from the tower at a distance of more than 30 mi. (50km). It was made up of three stories and built out of stone blocks, which were later reinforced with lead. It was decorated with statues of Triton, the mythical sea messenger of the Greeks, and was later topped by a statue of Triton's father, Poseidon, god of the oceans (or possibly Zeus, father of all the gods). The great lighthouse stood for almost 1,500 years, but it finally collapsed into ruin during an earthquake in A.D. 1303. It was destroyed by a second tremor in 1323, becoming the last of the six lost wonders of the ancient world to disappear.

▲ The Pharos was approached by a ramp and had a central shaft for fuel and maintenance. The lower section was square, the middle section was eight-sided, and the top section was round. It was so famous that in many languages the word for "lighthouse" comes from "Pharos"—for example, the French word is *phare*.

▶ In the 1990s marine archaeologists from France began to investigate the harbor in Alexandria. They found evidence from many different periods of Egyptian history, including some massive blocks of stone that probably came from the original Pharos. Some were inscribed with Greek letters. Here, diver Jean-Yves Empereur examines earlier underwater remains.

SUMMARY OF CHAPTER 1: SEVEN ANCIENT WONDERS

Helios, the sun god, in whose honor the Colossus of Rhodes was erected.

The world of the Greeks

The ancient Greeks were great travelers. Their homeland lay in the region of the eastern Mediterranean. Around 2,800 years ago they also began to settle in many other lands around southern Europe and western Asia. By 323 B.C., the Macedonian ruler Alexander the Great had led Greek armies across much of Asia and into Egypt as well. The ancient Greeks loved to talk and write about the incredible sights that they had seen on their travels.

The writers

A trend emerged among Greek authors to list the seven places that they thought were the most wonderful of all. These writers included Herodotus (484–420 B.C.), Callimachus of Cyrene (305–240 B.C.), and the poet Antipater of Sidon, who lived in around 120 B.C. A famous text called "About the Seven Wonders of the World" was probably written in the A.D. 500s.

The Seven Wonders

The list of wonders of the world varied from one writer to another, although there is agreement about the following:
1 The Great Pyramid in Giza, Egypt, was built for the death of the pharaoh Khufu in 2566 B.C.
2 Babylon, and perhaps its Hanging Gardens, were in Mesopotamia (present-day Iraq). Babylon was certainly rebuilt during the reign of Nebuchadnezzar II (605–562 B.C.).
3 The majestic statue of the god Zeus in Olympia, Greece, was erected around 430 B.C.
4 The Artemisium in Ephesus (now Turkey) was also completed in around 430 B.C.
5 The original Mausoleum was the most impressive tomb of its day. It was built in Halicarnassus in c. 350 B.C.
6 The Colossus was a gigantic statue of Helios, the sun god, erected close to the harbor of Rhodes around 280 B.C.
7 The Pharos (c. 290 B.C.) was a landmark and beacon that marked the entrance to the port of Alexandria in Egypt.

Go further . . .

Read more about the seven wonders of the ancient world at:

http://ce.eng.usf.edu/pharos/wonders/list.html

Kingfisher Knowledge: Life in Ancient Rome by Simon Adams (Kingfisher, 2005)

Eyewitness Guide: Ancient Egypt by George Hart (Dorling Kindersley, 2002)

Voyages Through Time: Ancient Greece by Peter Ackroyd (DK Children, 2006)

Mesopotamia: What Life Was Like in Ancient Sumer, Babylon, and Assyria (Find Out About) by Lorna Oakes (Southwater, 2004)

Archaeologist
Investigates ancient remains and ruins of buildings in order to find out how people lived in the past.

Curator
Takes care of the ancient treasures and collections that are kept in museums and manages the exhibitions.

Diver
Investigates underwater wrecks and archaeological sites such as that of the Colossus of Rhodes or the Pharos in Alexandria.

Egyptologist
An archaeologist who specializes in the study of the buildings and way of life of ancient Egypt.

Visit the Giza pyramids, in Cairo, Egypt.
Contact:
The Egyptian Office of Tourism
Abbassia Square
Cairo, Egypt
Phone: +20 (0)285 4509/284 1970
http://www.egypt.travel/type12.php?page=home

To see fabulous treasures from Egypt and ancient Greece, visit:
The British Museum
London, England WC1B 3DG, U.K.
Phone: +44 (0)20 7323 8299
www.thebritishmuseum.ac.uk

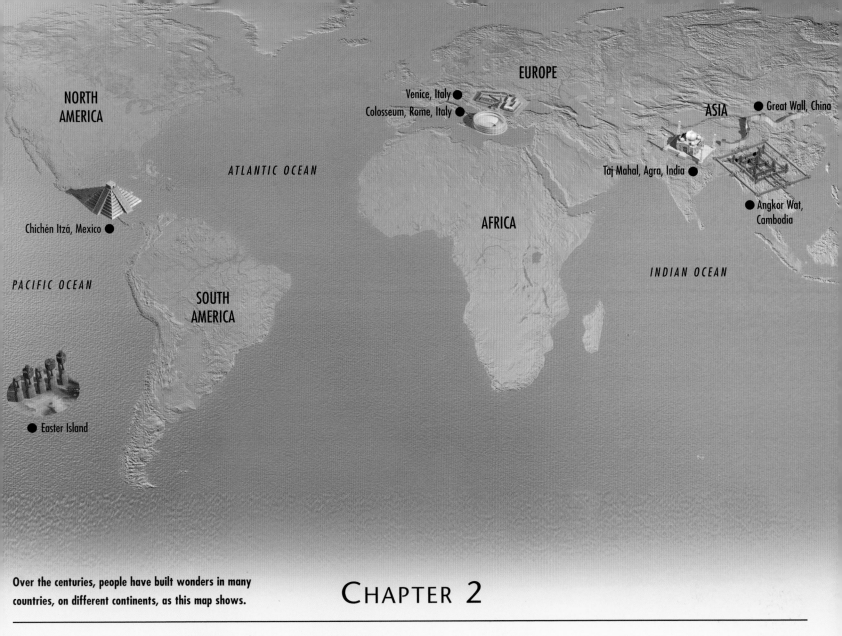

NORTH
AMERICA

ATLANTIC OCEAN

Chichén Itzá, Mexico ●

PACIFIC OCEAN

SOUTH
AMERICA

● Easter Island

EUROPE

Venice, Italy ●
Colosseum, Rome, Italy ●

AFRICA

INDIAN OCEAN

ASIA

● Great Wall, China

Taj Mahal, Agra, India ●

● Angkor Wat,
Cambodia

Over the centuries, people have built wonders in many countries, on different continents, as this map shows.

CHAPTER 2

The wider world

The wonders of the ancient world did not, of course, include places that were unknown to ancient Greek geographers. At the time, there were already remarkable sights to be seen in northern Europe, India and China, Africa, and the Americas. In medieval Europe, where scholars loved to make numbered lists of everything they could, there were constant revisions of the ancient lists. What about prehistoric sites, such as the mysterious stones that were raised in Stonehenge in southern England in around 2000 B.C.? And surely the Hagia Sophia, the great Christian church in Constantinople built in A.D. 537, was the wonder of its age. There was no shortage of suggestions, but no definitive list could be made, since it would immediately be overtaken by new marvels—a few of which may be seen on the following pages.

Colosseum in Rome

Imagine a crowd of 50,000 excited people pouring into a huge, oval-shaped building through 80 entrances. See them sweltering on the terraces in the heat of the day. Hear the braying trumpets and the incredible roar of the crowd as it booms and echoes across the city. This is not a modern sports stadium or a rock concert— it is Rome in the year A.D. 100. The building is the Flavian Amphitheater, known to later generations as the Colosseum.

▼ The cruel "games" that were held in Roman amphitheaters were so popular that they were sponsored by many emperors. It was not until A.D. 326 that the games were finally closed down. The great stone blocks of the Flavian Amphitheater still stand today in the center of Rome, Italy. A visitor today can easily see why the building became known as the Colosseum because of its colossal size.

▼ Rome's Flavian Amphitheater opened for business in A.D. 80. It measured 1,729 ft. (527m) around its perimeter and was 187 ft. (57m) high. Over the years it was filled with the latest technology, allowing for the central area to be flooded or cages of wild animals to rise up into the arena from the network of rooms below, as if by magic. Sailors were employed to rig up canvas awnings as shade for the crowds.

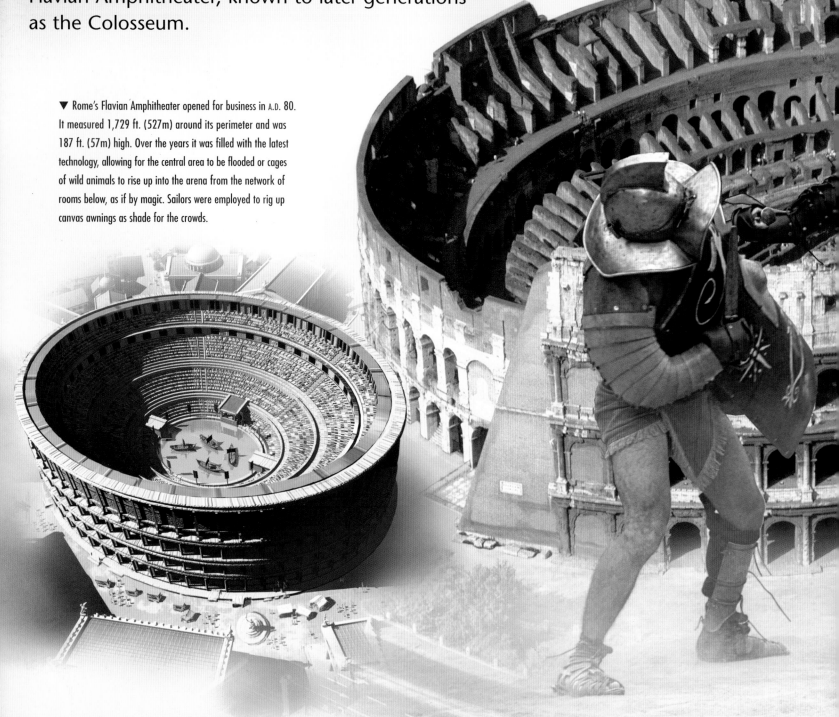

Engineering genius

If the Greeks of 300 B.C. had been able to see the amazing engineering feats achieved by the Romans 400 years later, they would have had to rewrite their lists of world wonders. The four-story-high Colosseum was spectacular. It could be completely flooded to stage mock naval battles. And the arena could be filled with dazzling white sand—in fact, *arena* is the Latin word for "sand."

◀ Gladiators were divided into various classes of combatants. Some fought with short swords and special helmets, others fought with nets and tridents or with daggers. It was thought at the time that this type of fighting would educate young Romans and encourage them to become tough and brave.

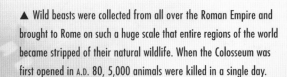

▲ Wild beasts were collected from all over the Roman Empire and brought to Rome on such a huge scale that entire regions of the world became stripped of their natural wildlife. When the Colosseum was first opened in A.D. 80, 5,000 animals were killed in a single day.

Savage "entertainment"

Other wonders are monuments to humanity's most noble ideals, but the Colosseum was a monument to unspeakable cruelty. The crowds came to this arena to see blood spill. There were fights between wild animals, with lions encouraged to attack giraffes or camels. There were staged "hunts," in which people slaughtered large numbers of wild animals. Sometimes, prisoners would be thrown to the beasts, and the crowd would laugh as they watched them being devoured by tigers or crocodiles.

The gladiators

One of the most popular spectacles of all of those seen in the Colosseum were the fights to the death between gladiators. These were trained fighters, often slaves or ex-prisoners, although some were volunteers. If the crowd believed that a gladiator had fought bravely, they might appeal to the patron of the games—perhaps the emperor himself for the gladiator's life to be spared. If the crowd thought that the gladiator had been cowardly, they would demand that he die. Most gladiators had short lives, but successful ones became celebrities and were offered their freedom.

Great Wall of China

The world's longest wall snakes across northern China, crossing mountains and deserts. It stretches from Gansu in the west to the eastern coast. The Chinese call it *wanli changcheng*, the "Great Wall of 10,000 Leagues." The main wall is around 2,145 mi. (3,460km) long, with an extra 1,770 mi. (2,860km) of branches and spurs. Today many sections lie in ruins. The best-preserved part is north of the capital, Beijing.

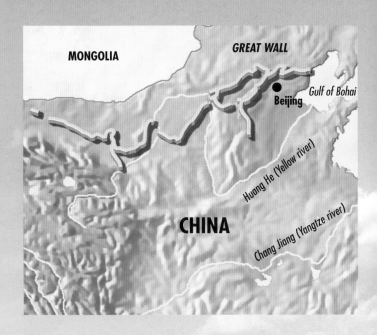

▼ Mongol horsemen, led by the great warrior Temujin, or Genghis Khan ("universal ruler"), rode through the ancient defenses of the Great Wall to conquer most of northern China between A.D. 1211 and 1223. They went on to rule all of China until 1368.

▼ During the 1300s and 1400s, China was still under constant threat of invasion. This part of the wall was built during that period. Roadways and steps were built along the top of the wall, allowing messengers and soldiers armed with crossbows to travel quickly.

▲ The incredible length of the Great Wall is made clear on this map of China. A network of defenses, dating from many different periods of Chinese history, stretches from the central Asian steppes to the Pacific Ocean. The most visited section of the Great Wall is in Badaling, close to Beijing.

Defending the land

From 453 to 221 B.C., the Chinese people were divided. They lived in separate kingdoms, and their rulers fought endless wars against each other. Some territories were also attacked by fierce raiders from the north, the Xiongnu. Huge earthworks were constructed to keep these nomadic warriors out of Chinese lands. In 221 B.C. Qin Shi Huangdi, the ruler of the Qin kingdom, became the first emperor. He united China and sent soldiers, slaves, and peasants to the far north to build new defenses. They built walls of rubble, brick, and stone, with strong foundations—the beginnings of the Great Wall.

▲ Watchtowers were built at regular intervals along the Great Wall. They were up to 40 ft. (12m) tall and could be used as lookouts or fortresses and housing garrisons of troops and stockpiled supplies. They also served as signal stations, using beacons, smoke, or flags for messages or to warn of invasions.

Rulers and invaders

During the following centuries, the Great Wall was built on and repaired, before parts fell into ruin once again. It provided a useful route for trade, but most rulers discovered that it was inefficient and expensive to maintain. In A.D. 1215 China was overrun by a new enemy from the north, the Mongols, who rode through gaps in the defenses. The last great phase of wall-building took place under the Ming emperors, who ruled China from 1368 to 1644.

The greatest wonder

European travelers in China were awestruck by the Great Wall. In the 1660s Ferdinand Verbiest, a Flemish priest and scientist, reported that "the seven wonders of the world put together are not comparable to this work." In modern times the Great Wall has become a symbol of China—its glorious ancient history and its engineering genius.

Angkor Wat

In 1860 a French naturalist named Henri Mouhot was exploring the jungles of Cambodia, in southeast Asia. Underneath a tangle of creepers and tree roots, he discovered an extraordinary group of ancient buildings. Archaeologists began work there and soon uncovered the lost world of the Khmer people.

The past revealed

As the vegetation was stripped away by the archaeologists, the buildings of the medieval Khmer civilization came into view. They belonged to the capital Angkor Thom, dating back to around A.D. 1200. A short distance to the south, Mouhot noted the existence of a temple. He described it as greater than "anything left to us by Greece or Rome." Angkor Wat (meaning "temple") was less overgrown by the jungle, but it still took many years of hard work to clear it from the surrounding vegetation.

▲ This relief carved in stone from the eastern gallery in Angkor Wat shows a famous image of the Hindu god Vishnu with the god Indra above him. The Angkor Wat temple was dedicated to Vishnu.

▼ Angkor Wat is the most impressive of 100 stone temples surviving around the modern Cambodian town of Siem Reap. In medieval times there would also have been several wooden buildings in the area.

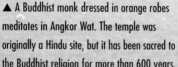

▲ A Buddhist monk dressed in orange robes meditates in Angkor Wat. The temple was originally a Hindu site, but it has been sacred to the Buddhist religion for more than 600 years.

Temple of the five towers

The area that includes the temple of Angkor Wat is the largest religious site on Earth, with an area of 403 acres (163 hectares). The temple had been founded in around A.D. 1150 to mark the funeral of Suryavarman II. This king had been the ruler of the Khmer people, and also a Hindu. He was devoted to the god Vishnu, in whose honor the temple was built and to whom it was dedicated. Angkor Wat's five sandstone towers were created to represent the peaks of Mount Meru, the home of the gods in Hindu mythology. The site was enclosed by a wall that was two miles (3.6km) long, with a moat. It has three long, rectangular galleries, one above the other, as well as terraces and many beautiful statues and reliefs.

Changes in fortune

The impressive temple later became a center for the Buddhist religion, attracting many pilgrims. However, it was abandoned in the 1430s after attacks on it by the Tai people from the south. Around 90 percent of Cambodians today are of Khmer descent, and Angkor Wat has become a symbol of their ancient culture. The temple's status as a world wonder is confirmed by the visits there of more than one million tourists each year. These tourists, however, may do more damage to the site by simply walking around it than the jungle ever did.

▶ Henri Mouhot's discovery led to the uncovering of many artistic treasures. This serene head is one of those carved in the stone towers of the Bayon, a marvelous temple built in the center of Angkor Thom by King Jayavarman VII in around 1200. He was a Buddhist and a powerful ruler.

Pacific Ocean mysteries

Easter Island, or Rapa Nui, is one of the most remote spots on Earth. It lies in the South Pacific Ocean, around 2,232 mi. (3,600km) west of the coast of Chile. Guarding this small island, which is dotted with extinct volcanoes, are gigantic heads made out of carved stone. Almost 1,000 heads gaze out over the rolling hills, but their origins are shrouded in mystery.

The seafarers

Between around 1500 B.C. and A.D. 1200, the islands of the South Pacific Ocean were settled by the Polynesian people, who originated in southeast Asia. These seafarers traveled in canoes with sails and were skilled navigators. Easter Island was the easternmost point of their travels and may have been reached, probably from the Marquesas Islands, as early as A.D. 400. The first Europeans to discover the island were the Dutch, on Easter Sunday in 1722.

▲ A woman in traditional Polynesian dress dances in Ahu Tongariki on Easter Island. This coastal site is in the southeast of the island. It has some of the most massive *moai* of this remote spot. All of them were quarried from the extinct volcano of Rano Raraku. Ahu Tongariki was devastated by a tsunami (a gigantic wave caused by an earthquake) in 1960. The giant heads have since been put back into position by archaeologists.

Giant statues

Easter Island's strange statues, called *moai*, were probably carved by the islanders between around A.D. 1000 and 1600. Some of the *moai*, which have noble faces with curved noses and long earlobes, were arranged in rows on ceremonial stone platforms called *ahu*. Some have *pukau*—cylindrical stone "topknots," which may originally have been painted dark red. Others have hands with long fingers that rest across their stomach, and many have deep eye sockets, which archaeologists believe may have been filled with coral.

Figures of power

The statues weigh up to 84 tons, and some tower more than 36 ft. (11m) tall. They probably represented ancestral chiefs and were believed to have great spiritual power. Carving, moving, and erecting the *moai* must have been skilled work that took several years. Almost 900 *moai* have been traced so far, some toppled over and others re-erected. Around 600 still lie uncompleted, many in the quarry where they were being prepared.

▲ This is the ruin of a typical house in Ahu Tahai, in the east of the island. Its outer stones form the shape of a boat and would have supported arches made out of timber. On the land surrounding their homes the Easter Islanders grew sweet potatoes, yams, sugar cane, and bananas, and they also raised chickens.

◄ The slopes of Rano Raraku are dotted with *moai*, gazing back into an unknown past. The thriving culture of Easter Island rapidly declined after A.D. 1600. Some historians believe that the islanders cut down too many trees, destroying the environment that supported them. Others think that it was because clans fought bitterly for scarce resources. Further disasters struck in the 1800s, when slave traders took away 35 percent of the island's population to work as laborers or servants in Peru.

Chichén Itzá

The ancient Greeks who wrote up the original lists of the wonders of the world knew nothing about the Americas. When Europeans finally traveled through Mexico and Peru in the 1500s, they could hardly believe their eyes. There they found ancient cities, pyramids, and temples, as well as great treasuries of gold, silver, and jade. Several peoples were the creators of these great works, particularly the Maya, the Toltecs, the Aztecs, and the Incas.

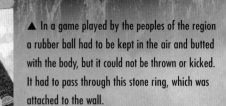

▲ In a game played by the peoples of the region a rubber ball had to be kept in the air and butted with the body, but it could not be thrown or kicked. It had to pass through this stone ring, which was attached to the wall.

◀ The game was part of a religious ritual, played in honor of the gods. The ball court at Chichén Itzá was the largest Mayan ball court, measuring 308 ft. by 115 ft. (94m by 35m).

◀ A stone figure lies on its back, holding a dish. Several of these stone statues, known as *chacmools*, were discovered in Chichén Itzá and elsewhere in the region. They may be associated with human sacrifices that were made to the rain god Chac.

Who built the city?

Many of the most remarkable Mexican sites are on the Yucatán Peninsula. This region is flat, hot, and very dry, except for small, sunken lakes called *cenotes*. It was close to three of these precious water supplies that a settlement called Chichén Itzá was founded by the Itzá, a Mayan people who had migrated to the region. By A.D. 600, Chichén Itzá had grown into a city. In around 987 it was probably conquered by a Toltec invader, because there is a mixture of Mayan and Toltec-style stonework from this period. After wars among the Maya in the 1200s, the city fell into ruin.

Warriors and skulls

The ruins of Chichén Itzá still stand today. Within an area of 4 sq. mi. (10km²), there are temples and terraces, stepped pyramids and stairways, altars, palaces, thrones, baths, ball courts, inscriptions, marketplaces, an observatory, and carvings of the gods. The massive Temple of Warriors, bordering the jungle, is surrounded by 60 pillars. Carved in its stone are Toltec warriors with pierced noses, ready to battle in feathers and headdresses. On the east terrace of the ball court are carved serpents and skulls. The grisly Wall of Skulls was once a place where heads were skewered during human sacrifices.

Ancient civilizations

The ancient peoples of Mexico regarded human sacrifices to the gods as a great honor for the victims. Civilizations such as the Maya did not have knowledge of metal tools or the wheel, but they did produce incredible buildings, jewelry, featherwork, pottery, textiles, and wall paintings. They invented calendars and ways of writing and studied the stars. Spanish soldiers invaded Mexico in 1519 and looted and destroyed many of the wonders that they found. However, today, the descendants of the Maya still live across a large area of Mexico and Central America.

▲ This pyramid has nine "steps," representing nine underground worlds, and stands 79 ft. (24m) high. Its 91 stairs lead to a temple dedicated to Kukulkán. This was not only the supposed name of the Toltec invader, but also of the plumed serpent god, also known as Quetzalcoatl. The Spanish called this pyramid the *Castillo*, or castle.

The Taj Mahal

Is this the most beautiful building in the world? The Taj Mahal overlooks the Yamuna river, close to Agra, in India. It is a mausoleum that was built between 1632 and 1653 by Shah Jahan, the Mogul emperor. The Moguls were Muslim rulers of most of India at the time. This masterpiece of architecture commemorates the emperor's wife, known as Mumtaz Mahal.

▲ Shah Jahan was born in Lahore (in modern-day Pakistan) in 1592. In 1612 he married Arjumand Bann Begum, who was famous for her beauty. He had several wives, but she was his favorite. She took the name Mumtaz Mahal, meaning "adornment of the palace," and bore him 14 children, seven of which survived childhood.

Marble and gemstones

The Mogul emperors encouraged the creation of beautiful art and architecture. After Mumtaz Mahal died in 1631, Shah Jahan assembled a workforce of more than 20,000 skilled men. The finest white marble was quarried, and precious stones— amethysts, jade, lapis lazuli, turquoise, coral, and mother-of-pearl— were imported from all over Asia to decorate the building. The precious stones were inlaid into the stonework in beautiful flower patterns. As the central building rose, towering arches appeared, designed in the Persian style. Verses from the Islamic scriptures, the Koran, adorned the walls in a flowing Arabic script.

Building paradise

Mumtaz Mahal was more than a wife and a mother. She was also Shah Jahan's closest friend and political adviser. When she died, it is said that he refused to eat for eight days. To reflect his devotion to her, he wanted to build the most beautiful monument. The Taj Mahal was topped with four canopies and a huge, gleaming white dome. Four soaring minarets, or prayer towers, flanked the tomb, and there was also a mosque and courtyards. The complex was set in a large formal Mogul garden divided into four parts, which included pools that reflected the image of the main building. The Taj Mahal was a monument to God, as well as to human love and grief. However, it also served to show off the power and wealth of Shah Jahan, although the expense of building it almost bankrupted the Mogul Empire.

▲ The tiles and inlays that decorate the Taj Mahal show Indian and Persian influences. The style is elaborate but subtle so that it does not distract the eye from the building as a whole.

◄ The beautiful stonework of the Taj Mahal has been threatened in modern times by air pollution from factories and city traffic and by the many tourists who visit the site.

The final days

It is said that Shah Jahan planned to build a matching mausoleum for himself in black stone. However, his plans were not successful. He became sick in 1658, and his four sons rebelled against him. One of them, Aurangzeb, gained control of the empire and, to cement his power, imprisoned his father in Agra Fort. Tended by Jahanara, his oldest daughter, Shah Jahan died there eight years later, in 1666, and was finally buried in the Taj Mahal next to Mumtaz Mahal. Today the Taj Mahal is the best-known image of India, shown in countless photographs gleaming in the moonlight or lit up by the dawn.

▼ Two Hindu women celebrate the festival of Diwali beside the pools of the Taj Mahal. Hindus, Muslims, and people of all religions are inspired by this sublime building.

Canals of Venice

The cities of Europe have produced many wonders in the last 1,000 years. There are soaring medieval cathedrals with beautifully colored stained-glass windows, mighty castle towers, and strong city walls, as well as lavish palaces containing incredible paintings and tapestries by the most talented artists. One of the most inspiring cities of all is Venice, in Italy, with its canals and waterways instead of roads. It is a city that was built on a group of low-lying islands, and to a visitor it looks as if it has risen directly out of the sea.

▲ Central Venice is made up of 118 little islands, connected to each other by around 400 bridges. Between them is a maze of waterways and canals. This aerial photograph shows the giant loop of the Grand Canal in the heart of the city.

The town that was built on water

In ancient times the coast around Venice was marshy. A shallow lagoon was protected from the open sea by little islands and sandbanks. Refugees from the mainland settled there in the A.D. 400s, when Italy was being repeatedly invaded. Surprisingly, the refugees prospered. They collected salt, they fished, they built ships, and they made glass. Above all, they traded. In the Middle Ages merchants from Venice controlled trade with Asia, importing precious silks and spices. To build the foundations for a new city, they sank millions of timber poles into the soggy ground.

A life on the water

By the 1400s, Venice had become one of the richest cities in the world. At its peak it had 36,000 sailors moving more than 3,000 ships in and out of its harbor. During the following centuries, splendid bridges, markets, boatyards, palaces, and churches were built. However, there were few roads. Venetians preferred to travel by boat along a network of beautiful canals. Venice was a significant port. The Venetians knew that they depended on the sea, and each year this was confirmed in a public ceremony. The leader of the city, the Doge, was rowed out to sea in a golden galley. He threw a ring into the waves, making the declaration that the city was wedded to the sea.

▼ At street level it is all water, so the easiest way to travel is by boat. Today motorboats and water buses, called *vaporetti*, maneuver through the canals, but for many tourists the only way to travel is by gondola (below). This is the traditional, black-painted boat of the canals, with a narrow hull more than 36 ft. (11m) long and an upturned prow and stern. The gondola is propelled by a gondolier holding a long oar.

▶ A flood flows down the Piazetta into Saint Mark's Square in the center of Venice, stranding the chairs and tables that are normally occupied by tourists. The grand building is the Doge's Palace, the medieval center of government. The architecture shows influences of both Asia and Europe, a reminder of the city's trading heritage. Venice is used to flooding, but there are serious concerns for the future safety of the city.

The "most serene" city

Venice began to decline as a political power at the end of the 1700s. However, it remained a center of art, music, and theater, with an elegant carnival that is still held every year. Venice became famous as *La Serenissima*, the "most serene" of cities. It still attracts many visitors. No one can ever forget the sight of the city's skyline appearing for the first time above the pale blue waters of the lagoon or the streets that are made of water. However, Venice's future is under threat. Sea levels are rising, and floods there are becoming more common. It is a fragile city, requiring many difficult planning decisions if its precious buildings and treasures are to be saved.

SUMMARY OF CHAPTER 2: THE WIDER WORLD

There are around 1,000 gigantic stone heads on Easter Island in the southern Pacific Ocean.

Rome and beyond

The ancient Greeks only knew about southern Europe, western Asia, and north Africa. Beyond the limits of their world were distant, unknown lands, all with their own mysteries and wonders. By 2,000 years ago, Roman power was expanding and Roman engineers were building roads, aqueducts, and great cities. The Colosseum in Rome was opened in A.D. 80. It was an impressive architectural achievement.

The world opens up

For 1,200 years after the collapse of the Roman Empire in A.D. 476, beautiful buildings and monuments were created on almost every continent. These became more widely known as a great age of world exploration began in the 1300s and 1400s. Moroccans and Venetians traveled to China, Chinese traders traveled to Arabia and east Africa, and European sailors reached the Americas.

From China to Mexico

The most impressive Chinese monument is the Great Wall, built over hundreds of years to keep out invaders. One of the world's largest religious sites is the magnificent Angkor Wat, in Cambodia, constructed in around A.D. 1150. The most mysterious of all of the world wonders are the *moai*, gigantic stone heads erected on remote Easter Island, in the Pacific Ocean, from A.D. 1000 to 1600. Before the European discovery of the Americas in 1492, the Maya, Toltecs, Aztecs, and Incas were building great cities and temples. Chichén Itzá in Mexico thrived from A.D. 600 to 1200.

Grace and beauty

The most beautiful of the later world wonders could possibly be the Taj Mahal, a mausoleum built by the Mogul emperor of India for his wife, finished in 1652. Europe's great cities—Paris, Florence, and London—are full of treasures. One of the most glorious cities is Venice, erected on low-lying islands in an Italian lagoon—truly a city built on water.

Go further . . .

Read more about the amazing wonders of the wider world:
http://www.metmuseum.org /toah/hd/eais/hd_eais.htm
http://www.venetia.it/
http://www.mysteriousplaces.com/ mayan/TourEntrance.html

Great Structures in History: The Great Wall of China by Rachel Lynette (KidHaven Press, 2004)

Great Buildings: The Taj Mahal by Christine Moorcroft (Steck-Vaughn, 1997)

Secrets in Stone: All About Maya Hieroglyphs by Laurie Coulter and Sarah Jane English (Scholastic, Inc., 2004)

Anthropologist
Studies the development of human cultures, customs, and beliefs.

Art historian
Studies old pictures, carvings, designs, and sculptures.

Conservationist
Takes care of old buildings and sites, keeping them in good condition and protecting them.

Sinologist
Studies the history, culture, and languages of China.

Stonemason
Cuts, carves, and finishes stone that is used in buildings and restorations.

Explore the Colosseum, the battleground of the gladiators:
Piazza del Colosseo
Rome, Italy
Phone: +39 06 39967700
www.the-colosseum.net/idx-en.htm

Learn about Angkor Wat and endangered sites on the History Channel:
www.history.com/classroom/unesco/ angkor/index2.html

Discover more about Chichén Itzá and other Central American wonders:
www.mnsu.edu/emuseum/archaeology /sites/meso_america/chichenitza.html

Learn more about Oriental architecture:
www.orientalarchitecture.com/agra/ tajmahalindex.htm

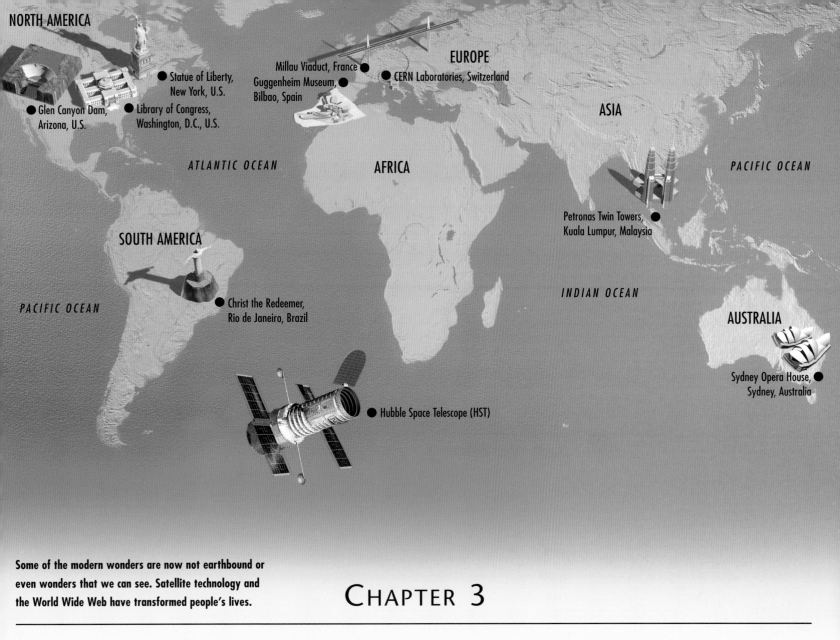

NORTH AMERICA

● Statue of Liberty,
New York, U.S.

Millau Viaduct, France ●
Guggenheim Museum, ●
Bilbao, Spain

EUROPE

● CERN Laboratories, Switzerland

● Glen Canyon Dam,
Arizona, U.S.

● Library of Congress,
Washington, D.C., U.S.

ATLANTIC OCEAN

AFRICA

ASIA

PACIFIC OCEAN

SOUTH AMERICA

Petronas Twin Towers, ●
Kuala Lumpur, Malaysia

PACIFIC OCEAN

INDIAN OCEAN

AUSTRALIA

● Christ the Redeemer,
Rio de Janeiro, Brazil

Sydney Opera House, ●
Sydney, Australia

● Hubble Space Telescope (HST)

Some of the modern wonders are now not earthbound or
even wonders that we can see. Satellite technology and
the World Wide Web have transformed people's lives.

CHAPTER 3

Modern wonders

In the 1700s and 1800s Europe and North
America saw a rush of scientific and
technical advances—the Industrial Revolution.
There were astonishing inventions such as
steamships, trains, and cars. However, in
the 1900s newer styles of buildings were
designed, using concrete, steel, and glass.
Soaring skyscrapers took over cities. By
this century, many of humanity's ancient
dreams had come true: people could fly
and travel through space; they could build
incredible dams and bridges. The United
States Library of Congress could house
more than 29 million books. The World
Wide Web could provide access to almost
unlimited information around the globe.
Space telescopes could see to the ends of
the universe. Which ones of these marvels
will be counted as lasting wonders? Only
future generations will be able to tell.

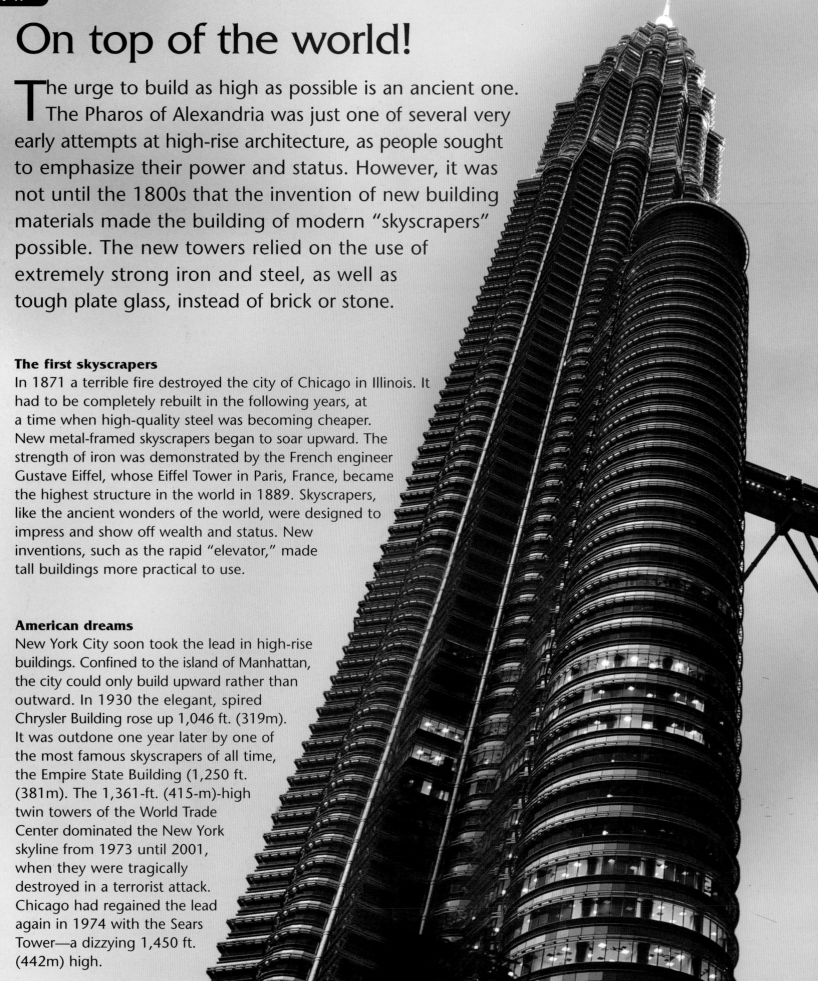

On top of the world!

The urge to build as high as possible is an ancient one. The Pharos of Alexandria was just one of several very early attempts at high-rise architecture, as people sought to emphasize their power and status. However, it was not until the 1800s that the invention of new building materials made the building of modern "skyscrapers" possible. The new towers relied on the use of extremely strong iron and steel, as well as tough plate glass, instead of brick or stone.

The first skyscrapers

In 1871 a terrible fire destroyed the city of Chicago in Illinois. It had to be completely rebuilt in the following years, at a time when high-quality steel was becoming cheaper. New metal-framed skyscrapers began to soar upward. The strength of iron was demonstrated by the French engineer Gustave Eiffel, whose Eiffel Tower in Paris, France, became the highest structure in the world in 1889. Skyscrapers, like the ancient wonders of the world, were designed to impress and show off wealth and status. New inventions, such as the rapid "elevator," made tall buildings more practical to use.

American dreams

New York City soon took the lead in high-rise buildings. Confined to the island of Manhattan, the city could only build upward rather than outward. In 1930 the elegant, spired Chrysler Building rose up 1,046 ft. (319m). It was outdone one year later by one of the most famous skyscrapers of all time, the Empire State Building (1,250 ft. (381m). The 1,361-ft. (415-m)-high twin towers of the World Trade Center dominated the New York skyline from 1973 until 2001, when they were tragically destroyed in a terrorist attack. Chicago had regained the lead again in 1974 with the Sears Tower—a dizzying 1,450 ft. (442m) high.

► These construction workers are taking a lunch break on an exposed steel beam 800 ft. (245m) above the ground! They are not wearing safety harnesses or hard hats. The year is 1932, and they are working on the 872-ft. (266-m)-high RCA Building, in New York's Rockefeller Center. The skyscraper is known today as the General Electric (GE) Building.

◄ Today each new skyscraper sensation is soon overtaken by another, as every city around the world competes. The Petronas Twin Towers (1,483 ft., or 452m), in Kuala Lumpur, Malaysia, held the record from 1998 to 2004.

Concrete and steel
Skyscraper design brought in a whole new range of building methods. Concrete was "reinforced" with steel rods. Huge pieces of concrete could be laid down as support for the foundations, or tough piles could be drilled deep down into the rock. Buildings were assembled around a central core. Planning on such a huge scale was a difficult job, and it created all types of environmental concerns. Projects needed computer modeling and even, like aircraft, testing in wind tunnels. New materials mean that recent skyscrapers have all types of incredible shapes and finishes.

| 1,053 ft. (321m) 1889 Eiffel Tower, Paris, France | 1,250 ft. (381m) 1931 Empire State Building, New York, U.S. | 1,483 ft. (452m) 1998 Petronas Twin Towers, Kuala Lumpur, Malaysia | 1,670 ft. (509m) 2003 Taipei 101, Taiwan | 1,814 ft. (553m) 1976 CN Tower, Toronto, Canada | unfinished 2005 Burj, Dubai, U.A.E |

▲ The height of skyscrapers, and also the height of free-standing structures, such as broadcasting towers, has continued to rise at a bewildering rate for more than 100 years. In 1931 the Empire State Building was more than twice the height of the Singer Building, which had astounded New Yorkers only 23 years earlier. By 2003, the pagodalike Taipei 101 in Taiwan had reached the dizzying height of 1,670 ft. (509m), and it had to be specially protected against earthquakes and tropical storms. Its elevators can take people up to the viewing station on the 89th floor at a speed of 39mph (63km/h). The Burj Dubai, under construction since 2005, is expected to be even higher than the Taipei 101. All of these buildings are extraordinary feats of engineering, but it remains to be seen which ones capture the public imagination and qualify as wonders of the world.

Architecture and the arts

In the last 100 years architects around the world have created incredible new cities, full of public buildings that inspire and provoke the imagination. Some of these are concert halls or art galleries, and others are offices or libraries. They have been given shape by exciting new technologies, including computer modeling and the creation of amazing new materials such as plastics, plate glass, steel, and reinforced concrete.

A temple of the arts
Bilbao is the main city of the Basque country—a region in Europe that extends from Spain into France. The Basque way of life has very ancient roots, but the newest addition to the architecture of Bilbao is a vision of the future. It is the Guggenheim Museum of Modern Art, which opened in 1997. The designer was an American, Frank Gehry, and the building's extraordinary curves and shapes were inspired by the lines of a ship.

Shells by the harbor

Another modern building, found on the other side of the world, is generally recognized as a new wonder. Just as ancient Greeks traveled to see the Great Pyramid in Egypt, today tourists flock to Australia to see this famous landmark, and new brides fly from as faraway as Japan to be photographed in front of its skyline. The Sydney Opera House is built on Bennelong Point in the city of Sydney, Australia, close to another famous landmark, the Sydney Harbour Bridge. The Opera House's ten roofs are shaped like giant seashells, or perhaps more like the billowing sails of the boats that cross the blue waters of the harbor below.

◀ Bilbao's Guggenheim Museum rises up magnificently from the Nervión river. It was made possible by computer modeling, which was able to look at the possibilities and limits of structures, stresses, shapes, and materials. The museum is built out of limestone, covered with plates of titanium like fish scales, and sheathed in glass.

▶ Many technological problems had to be overcome during the building of the Sydney Opera House. Public arguments about the design became very heated. Most people now agree that this is one of the landmark buildings of modern times.

A building to remember

The Sydney Opera House was designed by Danish architect Jørn Utzon and built between 1958 and 1973. The building complex covers an area of 4.5 acres (1.8 hectares) and is supported by 580 concrete piers, sunk deep underground. Inside there are more than 1,000 rooms, including theaters, studios, and concert halls. These rooms are used for opera, dance, theater, and all types of musical performances. The main concert hall can seat more than 2,500 people.

Water wonders

Water is essential for our survival on Earth. It allows people to drink, to irrigate crops, to use ships, and to generate power. Water can also pose a threat to life, for example, when the sea floods the land or when rivers break through their banks. The people who harness the power of water, or build defenses against flooding, have produced some of the most ingenious feats of engineering in modern times all around the world. Sometimes in very dangerous conditions and with great loss of life, they have built canals, irrigation systems, dams, and flood barriers.

▲ The cascade of more than two million cubic feet (62,000 m3) of water per second, thundering down the spillway of the Itaipu Dam, is an incredible sight. This massive hydroelectric scheme opened in 1984 on the borders of Brazil and Paraguay. Its turbines produce more electricity than ten nuclear power plants.

◀ Tugboats tow a ship through the Panama Canal in its early days. Thousands of workers died building this waterway between 1880 and its opening in 1914. It was one of the largest and most difficult engineering projects ever to have been undertaken. Today more than 14,000 ships pass through the canal each year. In 2006 plans were announced for a major new upgrade, allowing more and bigger ships to pass through.

The great canals

Humans have been building canals for at least 6,000 years. Many of these canals should be ranked as world wonders, including China's Grand Canal, completed in 1327. It is 1,104 mi. (1,781km) long, and at one point, it employed five million workers. The Suez Canal between the Red Sea and the Mediterranean Sea opened in 1869, allowing big ships to bypass the entire continent of Africa in their travels from east to west or vice versa. The year 1914 saw the opening of the Panama Canal in Central America, begun by the French and finished by the Americans. This waterway links the Atlantic and Pacific oceans and allows ships to avoid having to travel all the way around the tip of South America.

Dramatic dams

The 1900s were the great age of dam-building. The Grand Coulee Dam (1942), in Washington state, was built with almost 300 million cubic feet (80,000,000m^3) of concrete. The Aswan High Dam in Egypt, completed in 1970, contained 17 times as much rock as the pyramids in Giza, Egypt. The Rogun Dam (1990) in Tajikistan, in central Asia, soars to a height of 1,100 ft. (335m). The most incredible project of all is China's Three Gorges Dam, which should be operational by 2009. This will be the world's biggest generator of hydroelectric power and will also control floods on the Chang Jiang, the world's third-longest river.

Building for the future

Giant dams are mind-boggling wonders of the modern world, but they often cause real hardships—more than one million people have already been displaced from their homes by the Three Gorges Dam. Dams can also be disastrous for the environment. Perhaps engineering that will have the most lasting value will be schemes that protect people from rising sea levels. The world's biggest flood defenses are the Delta Scheme, an ongoing effort to prevent the waterlogged Dutch coast from being drowned by the North Sea. Since 1986, this amazing project has sealed off four major rivers with dams and barriers.

◄ This is the Glen Canyon hydroelectric power scheme, which dams the Colorado river in Arizona. Its rim curves around for an amazing 1,561 ft. (476m), and the base of its wall is 298 ft. (91m) thick. Opened in 1966, it is a perfect example of the strength and beauty of modern dams. However, like many dams, Glen Canyon has also been criticized for its impact on the environment and on the natural flow of the large river that feeds into it.

Building bridges

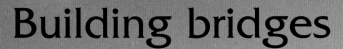

Bridges are structures that often combine incredible beauty with phenomenal strength. Some bridges are supported by curved arches, while others (beam bridges) are flat and rigid and supported by tall pillars (piers). Suspension bridges support the roadway (deck) with thick steel cables, slung from high towers. Many of these bridges are wonders of the modern age.

▼ Like threaded needles, the tapered pylons of the Millau Viaduct rise up from the misty valley of the Tarn river. There are seven of them in total, along 1.5 mi. (2.46km) of roadway. Each bridge section spans 1,148 ft. (350m), and the total weight of the steel deck is 36,000 tons.

◄ Building bridges is a delicate art. This is the Tsing Ma Suspension Bridge in Hong Kong, China. Its 4,517-ft. (1,377-m)-long deck carries both a road and a railroad. It is supported by steel cables that are suspended from 676-ft. (206-m)-high towers and anchored in to deep concrete at both ends of the bridge. The cables are spun over high iron saddles on top of each tower. Each main cable on the bridge is more than three feet (1m) thick and made up of 70,000 strands.

Tallest road bridge in the world

The Millau Viaduct opened in 2004. It carries traffic across the wide valley of the Tarn river, in southern France. The viaduct is a type of beam bridge, and its roadway rests on piers that extend upward as tall pylons. The deck is cable-stayed, which means that it is also held secure by powerful cables that fan out from the bridge's pylons. The biggest pylon soars to a height of 1,125 ft. (343m), making the Millau Viaduct the world's tallest road bridge. The road passes 876 ft. (267m) above the Tarn river, an altitude exceeded only by the 1,053-ft. (32-m)-high Royal Gorge Bridge in the Rocky Mountains of Colorado.

Famous bridges around the world

Many bridges are candidates for the title of modern wonders. One of the bridge systems that crosses Lake Pontchartain in the United States (1969) is more than 24 mi. (38km) long. The Akashi-Kaikyo Suspension Bridge in Japan has a single span of more than one mile (2km) and a total length of almost 2.5 mi. (3.9km). However, it is not always the highest or the longest bridges that are the best known or most loved by the public. The ornate Tower Bridge (1894), which can raise its deck to allow ships to pass through, has become a symbol of the city of London, England. In the U.S. the graceful Golden Gate Bridge (1937) is internationally famous as an emblem of the city of San Francisco.

Creating a wonder

Planning a massive bridge like the Millau Viaduct is a difficult task. Before it was built, various routes had to be considered. Which route would cause the least disruption to the town of Millau? Which route would be the least expensive to build? Which route would be the shortest? Which route would cause the least pollution and environmental damage? The combination of design, engineering, and architecture used to build this bridge was an international effort, involving the French, the British, and the Dutch. The final project took three years to build and employed 520 workers. It also used electronic labor, since the mechanics of the construction were carefully controlled by a computer.

▲ This is CERN, the headquarters of the multinational European Organization for Nuclear Research, which was founded in 1959. Scientists here devised the amazing World Wide Web in the 1990s. By coincidence, it is also a wonder of the world in its own right. Located on the French-Swiss border, it includes an underground tunnel that forms a circle that is 17 mi. (27km) long (indicated by the white line in this picture). This tunnel is used to research the nature of matter and nuclear particles.

The computer age

The first computers were developed in North America and Europe in the 1940s and 1950s. They were gigantic monsters, with large cables but little brainpower. They were only found in offices and in colleges. After the invention of the microchip, or integrated circuit, in 1958 and microprocessors in 1971, computers became smaller and smaller, but even more powerful. These changes led to the development of the first personal computers in the 1980s. People could now have the equivalent of several Alexandrian libraries in their own home, office, or laboratory. The computer revolution had completely changed the ways in which people lived and worked.

Info lab

Ever since humans first learned to write and record information, they have built centers where data could be stored and communicated. Around 4,000 years ago the palace of Ebla (today's Tell Mardikh in Syria) was one such place. Records that were kept there were written down on several thousand clay tablets and stored on shelves. The next center devised to house information technology was the library. One very famous library, which was founded by Ptolemy II in Alexandria, Egypt, in the 200s B.C., could store hundreds of thousands of manuscripts. Today the largest information and communication center that the world has ever known is available in your own living room. Its twin "wonders" are the Internet and the World Wide Web.

▶ Computer services are already interacting or merging with other types of communication media such as telephones, radios, televisions, newspapers, CDs, and DVDs. The electronic world that has been created in these ways is sometimes called cyberspace. It is an imaginary world, but it has a practical impact on everyday life. Today most businesses, schools, hospitals, and governments are dependent on computers. Cyberspace is like an extension of the human mind, since the computer must also arrange, classify, store, and process information.

Networks and webs

In 1983 colleges in the U.S. began to link up computer networks to aid communication. Other networks also began to connect, and this was the origin of the Internet—a global conglomeration that was made up of millions of networks. It could be used to carry E-mails and many other types of communication.

The most amazing information system using the Internet was the World Wide Web. This was developed in the early 1990s by English computer scientist Tim Berners-Lee and a group of other scientists at the nuclear physics research center, CERN, in Europe. They developed ways of linking documents using a language called hypertext. They also invented a whole system of web sites, browsers, and search engines.

Cyberspace

The computer was now no longer just a means of storing data. It was also a powerful research tool that, like the human brain, could follow up associations and connections. It could access a newspaper in Japan, a library in Australia, or a store in Italy, all in a matter of seconds. The traditional wonders of the world were real places or objects that people could visit, walk around, and touch. This new wonder had created a virtual world of its own, in cyberspace.

▼ Real libraries are still very necessary in the age of the World Wide Web. This beautiful library below is in Trinity College, Dublin, in Ireland. It has around four million books, many of which are very rare. The biggest modern library is the United States Library of Congress in Washington, D.C. It has 529 mi. (853km) of shelves, more than 29 million books, 2.7 million recordings, 12 million photographs, 4.8 million maps, and 58 million manuscripts. That certainly qualifies it as another wonder of the world.

Modern colossi

The Colossus of Rhodes may have disappeared long ago, but people are still fascinated and inspired by gigantic statues. Today's colossi often represent religious figures, such as Jesus Christ or the Buddha, or sometimes national heroes or political leaders. One massive female figure, in Volgograd, Russia, commemorates the Battle of Stalingrad, fought in 1942–1943. The statue was designed in 1967 and built out of concrete and steel. It is 270 ft. (82.3m) high and weighs more than 8,000 tons.

Christ the Redeemer
A statue of Jesus Christ with outstretched arms rises high above the city of Rio de Janeiro in Brazil. Completed in 1931, it is 125 ft. (38m) tall and built of reinforced concrete faced with weather-resistant soapstone. The statue stands on a 2,329-ft. (710-m) -high peak, Corcovado, on the outskirts of the city. The added height of the mountain makes this modern colossus the ultimate city landmark.

▼ Like any true wonder of the world, the 1,145-ton statue of Christ the Redeemer that towers over Rio de Janeiro has become the emblem of the city and of the whole country of Brazil. Its open arms, with a span of 98 ft. (30m), seem to embrace the world. Tourists can reach the base of the statue by road, rack-and-pinion railroad, or a hiking trail. The view over the sprawling city, the sparkling sea, distant hills, and mountain peaks is spectacular.

A symbol of liberty

With its crown of rays, its upheld torch, and its position at the approach to the harbor of New York City, the statue of "Liberty Enlightening the World" is clearly inspired by the ancient Colossus of Rhodes. The statue was inaugurated in 1886. Before the days of air travel, the Statue of Liberty was often the first thing that European immigrants and tourists traveling by ship saw as they approached the United States. The statue was a gift from the French people and was designed by the French sculptor Frédéric Auguste Bartholdi.

Story of a statue

Putting Liberty in place needed a feat of engineering, and the engineer who arranged it was Gustave Eiffel, who also built the famous Eiffel Tower in Paris, France. The Statue of Liberty was formed out of copper sheets, which were bolted to an iron framework. It was assembled in France between 1874 and 1884, shipped in pieces across the Atlantic Ocean, and erected on a small island in New York Harbor. The statue stands 305 ft. (93m) high, including the stone pedestal. Inside there are stairways leading up to the torch and a viewing platform in the crown.

▼ The raised torch on the Statue of Liberty symbolizes the spirit of freedom, a spirit that was shown by the people of America in the Revolutionary War of 1775–1783. This war saw Americans break away from British rule in order to found the United States. The rays in the statue's crown represent the seven oceans and seven continents. The monument is one of the most famous standing in the world today.

Reaching other worlds

The people who built the world's first wonders were fascinated by the sky at night. They built monuments that towered up to the heavens. They built observatories to study the movements of the planets and the stars. In the A.D. 1600s scientists began to use telescopes to study the sky more closely. Now, we can launch giant telescopes, such as the Hubble Space Telescope and the James Webb Space Telescope, to orbit our planet and scan the mysteries of deepest space.

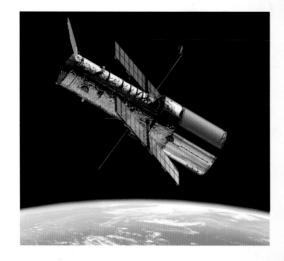

▲ The Hubble Space Telescope (HST) is a telescope that images rays of light. Its perfectly smooth main mirror measures 7.9 ft. (2.4m) across. More than 42 ft. (13m) long and weighing 11 tons, the spacecraft is powered by arrays of solar panels, which convert the Sun's rays into electricity. HST is now nearing the end of its life.

The Hubble Space Telescope investigates

In 1990 a new observatory was launched into orbit around Earth. It was named after the great American astronomer Edwin P. Hubble (1889–1953). The Hubble Space Telescope (HST) was programmed to circle the planet every 97 minutes. Doing this at a height of 357 ft. (575km) above Earth's surface, the HST was clear of the distorting effects of gases that are in Earth's atmosphere. At first the telescope had some problems, but these were fixed by space shuttle missions that linked up with the HST. Soon the observatory was sending breathtaking images of space back to Earth. Incredibly, HST has shown us new galaxies being born that are so far away that their light has taken 13.7 billion years to reach us. We are looking back almost to the origins of the universe itself.

A new space wonder

The United States National Aeronautics and Space Administration (NASA) plans to replace the Hubble Space Telescope with a new telescope that images mostly infrared rays, which have a longer wavelength than light. The new telescope will have a mirror that is 21 ft. (6.5m) in diameter. The James Webb Space Telescope (JWST) is scheduled to be launched in 2013, and it will operate around 930,000 mi. (1.5 million km) from its home planet. It will take three months to reach this distant orbit. JWST should be able to see back even farther than Hubble, giving us valuable information about how the universe was formed.

Other wonders, other worlds

Space telescopes are supported by all types of advanced telescopes and observatories back on Earth. Many telescopes scan the skies to pick up radio waves, which have longer wavelengths than infrared. Russia's RATAN 600 radio telescope is the world's biggest, with an antenna that is 1,889 ft. (576m) in diameter. The United States' Very Large Array (VLA) is made up of 27 units linked in a gigantic "Y" formation. Each unit has an 82-ft. (25-m)-long antenna. Spacecraft will continue to probe the secrets of space in the centuries to come—they may discover wonders that we can hardly imagine.

► The Hubble Space Telescope has sent hundreds of thousands of spectacular images from space back to Earth. It imaged M16, known as the "Eagle Nebula," in 2004. This nebula is a giant cloud of cold hydrogen and dust and is a breeding ground for new stars. The towering column seen here is believed to have a height of around 56 trillion mi. (90 trillion km).

◄ This is the incredible new space observatory, the James Webb Space Telescope (JWST). Its mission will be to seek images of the earliest galaxies being formed, in order to discover more about the formation of stars and planetary systems and to analyze planets to see if they are capable of supporting life.

SUMMARY OF CHAPTER 3: MODERN WONDERS

The Statue of Liberty in New York Harbor is truly a modern colossus.

Science and progress
The Industrial Age led to rapid changes in technology and the creation of new materials with many different applications such as plastics. In the 1900s new world wonders followed each other in quick succession, and most now served a useful purpose. People believed that science would set humanity on a course of steady progress.

Modern magic
By this century some of that faith in science and technology had been eroded. Many inventions had polluted the planet and used up its precious resources. Wars and famines had shown that nightmares could come true, as well as dreams. Even so, the marvels of this century would have seemed to be pure magic to our ancestors. What would an ancient Greek poet have thought of a laptop computer connected to the Internet?

New buildings
Where should we look for modern wonders of the world? Four of the seven ancient wonders were buildings, and modern architecture offers many options. Skyscraper mania began in the 1880s—Taipei 101 (2003) is currently the tallest at 1,670 ft. (509m) but is scheduled to be outstripped by the Burj Dubai project. The most exciting modern architecture often belongs to public buildings, including the Sydney Opera House (1973) in Australia and the Guggenheim Museum (1997) in Bilbao, Spain.

Reaching for the stars
The last 50 years have seen astonishing advances in the building of dams and bridges. Recent examples, such as the Millau Viaduct, are wonders of civil engineering, but massive dams, such as the Three Gorges Dam in China, may have a serious impact on the environment. The monuments that are possibly closest in spirit to the ancient wonders of the world are the modern colossi, such as Christ the Redeemer (1931) in Rio de Janeiro, Brazil. However, today perhaps the most incredible of all the wonders are the World Wide Web and the spacecraft that explore new worlds.

Go further . . .

There is no shortage of suggestions for modern wonders of the world:
http://ce.eng.usf.edu/pharos/wonders/pharos.html
http://wonderclub.com/WorldWonders/ModernWonders.html
http://www.asce.org/history/seven_wonders.cfm
http://www.travelersdigest.com/seven_modern_wonders.htm

Sky Boys: How They Built the Empire State Building by Deborah Hopkinson and James E. Ransome (Schwartz & Wade, 2006)

Building World Landmarks: The Sydney Opera House by Peggy J. Parks (Blackbirch Press, 2004)

Architect
Designs, plans, and supervises buildings of all types.

Astronomer
Studies stars, planets, and other space phenomena.

Civil engineer
Designs, plans, and supervises the construction of bridges, dams, and tunnels.

Construction worker
Builds buildings of all types, working with different materials and machines.

Discover more about modern wonders of the world and make up your own list:
http://worldvstore.com/modernwonders.htm

Find out about the largest waterways, biggest dams, and longest bridges of the modern world:
www.guinnessworldrecords.com

Discover all there is to know about tall buildings on the exhibition site at:
www.moma.org/tallbuildings

Find out what you can do to help UNESCO's World Heritage Organization take care of the wonders of the world:
http://whc.unesco.org

World heritage

The world has more than seven wonders. In fact, it has more than 700 wonders. These great buildings, monuments, and feats of engineering represent more than just part of our history. They are our heritage, something to be taken care of and preserved so that they can be passed down from generation to generation.

The Imperial Palace in Beijing, China (1420)

Why care?

Why do wonders of the world matter? Many are ancient ruins already, and others—however beautiful or interesting they may be—simply hold up modern development in our cities. Surely we should be more concerned with the present, rather than obsessed with how lives were lived in the past?

The fact is that these sites remain an inspiration. They show us not only what humans have achieved in the past, but what they are capable of creating in the future. They demonstrate arts, crafts, engineering skills, cooperation, and imagination, as well as a natural curiosity about human existence. Of course, many wonders also show the darker side of human nature. Medieval castles may look picturesque, but they were originally designed as centers from which kings and lords carried out warfare and oppression. However, there are also lessons to be learned from these monuments.

Under threat

Many heritage sites are endangered, and there are many threats to their survival. Some sites are at risk because, over hundreds of years, time and weather have eroded them—perhaps timbers have rotted or foundations have subsided. Many sites suffer from damage caused by earthquakes or warfare. In recent years rainfall has often become polluted by fumes from traffic exhaust or industrial emissions. This "acid rain" can eat away at materials, particularly ancient stone. Another threat comes from the development of cities. A palace or a temple may be dwarfed by new skyscrapers and hidden from view. Even when a site has been well preserved, it may suffer from the thousands of visitors who swarm over it every day.

Conserving heritage sites

Around the world local and national organizations take care of conservation and restoration. The United Nations Educational, Scientific, and Cultural Organization (UNESCO) registers World Heritage Sites. It oversees the conservation of these sites and provides emergency funding when it is necessary.

Rock-hewn chuches in Lalibela, Ethiopia (A.D. 900s to 1200s)

Central and eastern Europe

Central Europe has a rich history. In Poland, for example, the sites are varied, including wonders such as the grim castle of the medieval Teutonic knights in Malbork and the magnificent old city center of Krakow in the south. Two beautiful and historic cities are Prague, the capital of the Czech Republic, and Budapest, the capital of Hungary. Eastern Europe includes the splendors of Russia, as can be seen in the city of Saint Petersburg. The heart of Moscow, the Russian capital, is dominated by the red walls and the glittering domed churches within the Kremlin—the center of government.

Europe—west, north, and south

Conservation problems in Europe include pollution, urban development, and mass tourism. Even so, western Europe has some of the best-conserved heritage sites in the world. There are prehistoric monuments such as 4,000-year-old Stonehenge in England or the Altamira Caves in Spain. There are the magnificent remains of ancient Greece such as the Parthenon (447–432 B.C.)—the temple of the goddess Athena that towers over Athens, Greece. The mark of ancient Rome is everywhere. The triple-decker, 1,061-ft. (49-m)-high Pont du Gard in southern France is a combined viaduct and aqueduct, built by the Romans around A.D. 150.

Medieval Europe produced spectacular cathedrals such

The Parthenon (447–432 B.C.) on the Acropolis in Athens, Greece

The cathedral of Notre Dame de Paris (1160–1345), on the Île de la Cité in the heart of France's capital city, Paris.

as Chartres in France (1220) and Ulm in Germany (started in 1337)—the world's tallest church, with a 530-ft. (161.5-m)-high spire. Great castles were built all of the way across Europe. The Alhambra in Granada is a breathtaking fortification and Islamic palace, which was built in the days when the Moors ruled Spain.

Italy saw an amazing surge of creativity in the 1400s and 1500s. This Renaissance, or "rebirth," resulted in the building of elegant cities such as Florence and Siena. In northern Europe, in the Low Countries (now the Netherlands and Belgium), and in Scandinavia, merchants built their houses along busy canals or waterfronts so that they could import and export goods. The Industrial Revolution began in the British Isles, and there the heritage of the 1700s and 1800s has its own beauty—docks, tin mines, textile mills, potteries, and ironworks. Soon this industrial world would sprawl across northern Europe—and the northeastern United States.

Northern Africa

The extraordinary monuments in Egypt, such as the tombs in the Valley of the Kings, are known around the world. The massive statues in Abu Simbel, more than 3,200 years old, had to be rescued and moved from the dangers of the rising waters of Lake Nasser when the Aswan High Dam was being built in the 1960s. The rescue was planned by UNESCO. Less well known sites in northeast Africa include the obelisk of Aksum from the A.D. 300s, returned to Ethiopia in 2005 after it was carried off to Italy in 1937. Another Ethiopian site is Lalibela, the site of 13 medieval chuches made from solid rock.

North Africa's glories also include the medieval mosques and souks, or markets, of cities from Cairo in the east to Marrakech and Fez in the west. Even the sweltering wilderness of the Sahara has its treasures—4,000-year-old rock paintings in Tassili n'Ajjer in Algeria.

Central and southern Africa

South of the Sahara the main building materials were mud, thatch, and wood—practical but not durable. In Mali there is the trading town of Tombouctou (1400s), the Grand Mosque in Djenné (1907), and the traditional thatched huts, shaped like witches' hats, of the Dogon people. The perfection of the thatched hut tradition may be seen in the 19th-century palace tombs of the Buganda kings, in Kampala, Uganda.

A type of coral cement was a popular building material along east Africa's Swahili coast, where Africans, Arabs, and Persians traded in the Middle Ages. Mosques and dwellings with ornately carved wooden doors may be seen on islands such as Lamu in Kenya and Zanzibar in Tanzania. The most famous stone-built building in southern Africa is Great Zimbabwe, the remains of a walled citadel that dates back to the 1100s.

The Kinkaku temple, "Golden Pavilion" (1398), in Kyoto, Japan

Wonders of western Asia

The world's first civilizations emerged in western Asia. In Iran there are the ruins of Persepolis, the Persian Empire's capital in 518 B.C. Petra in Jordan is a hidden city in the desert, carved from sandstone cliffs during the A.D. first century. Sana'a, in Yemen, has unique houses and mosques from the A.D. 600s to the 1000s. In the mountainous Cappadocia region in Turkey there are amazing underground towns and villages and mazes of rock-hewn passages dating back to the A.D. 300s.

The fabulous heritage sites in western Asia have faced many dangers from very different directions recently. Jerusalem, a holy city to Jews, Muslims, and Christians, is split by violent political and religious divides in Israel. The ancient clay-built citadel of Bam, in Iran, was destroyed by an earthquake in 2003. And the Iraq War, which began in 2003, has already put many ancient and valuable Mesopotamian sites at risk.

▲ The Alhambra, "Red Castle" (1248–1354), in Granada, Spain

Central Asia and the steppes

The central Asian steppes, deserts, and mountains were home to nomadic peoples who had no permanent home, but who moved around according to the seasons. Their tents left little trace on the landscape. However, along the ancient trading routes from China to the west wealthy cities emerged, such as Samarqand, now in Uzbekistan, famed for its medieval mosques and observatory.

An example of the risks to monuments in central Asia occurred in Afghanistan's fascinating Bamyan Valley in 2001, when the Taliban government blew up two gigantic statues of the Buddha with explosives.

South Asian heritage

Travel south from Afghanistan to Pakistan, and there you will find sites such as the ancient ruins of Mohenjo-Daro (2500–1500 B.C.), a city that was built by the Indus Valley civilization. In Lahore there are the Shalimar Gardens and the Lahore Fort (A.D. 1566). India is a large country with many treasures. In Ajanta, in the Deccan, 28 Buddhist cave temples were carved out of rock between the 100s B.C. and the A.D. 600s. These were adorned with stone carvings and paintings. Southern India has many Hindu sites, such as the marvel of Konarak, a 13th-century temple to the sun god Surya. This was buried in sand for 200 years.

Traditional problems facing south Asian sites have included the hot climate, monsoon rains, and dense vegetation. More recent poblems include road building and the spread of towns, as well as an increase in tourism, for example, in Sri Lankan cities such as Kandy.

East Asian marvels

China has many heritage sites. In Beijing there are the Temple of Heaven and the old Imperial Palace, with its 800 halls (both built in 1420). In Xian there is the underground mausoleum of the first Chinese emperor, Qin Shi Huangdi, with a lifelike army modeled in terra-cotta and buried in 210 B.C. In Leshan is a colossus, a 233-ft. (71-m)-high Buddha carved from a cliff face between A.D. 713 and 803. Many Chinese temples were damaged during a period of political unrest in the 1960s. However, many of these have now been restored.

Japan is known for its ultramodern cities, but Kyoto has splendid shrines of the Shinto religion. In North Korea there are tombs from the ancient kingdom of Koguryo, and in South Korea there are many shrines and palaces. Thailand's historic city of Ayutthaya (A.D. 1351) is marked by towers and Buddhist monasteries. Indonesia's marvels include the 1,200-year-old Buddhist temple of Borobodur, on the island of Java.

North America old and new

The North American continent usually sticks out in our minds as a relatively modern continent. There are buildings

▲ The standing stones of Stonehenge, England (2500–2000 B.C.)

from the 15th-century early colonization by English and Spanish settlers and historic centers in the old French cities, including Québec in Canada and New Orleans in the state of Louisiana. However, our imagination is also captivated by the "American dream"—the great skyscrapers of the cities or modern colossi such as the heads of presidents carved on Mount Rushmore in South Dakota between 1927 and 1941.

Many sites in North America date back to an earlier age, to the Native American cultures that once dominated the continent. One important world heritage site is in Mesa Verde in Colorado, where pueblo-style dwellings built between the A.D. 500s and 1100s cling to the sides of cliffs.

Mexico and Central America

The most developed pre-Columbian (Aztec, Olmec, and Mayan) civilizations emerged farther the south, where great cities, such as the Aztec capital of Tenochtitlán (on the site of modern-day Mexico City), were built. There are many astounding archaeologial sites in this region—for example, Monte Albán in Mexico or the Mayan sites of Palenque in Mexico and Copán in Honduras.

Lost cities of South America

Great stone arches and walls may still be seen in Tiwanaku in Bolivia (600–1200), and they are a testament to the many ancient civilizations of South America. Chan Chan (850–1470), on the Peruvian coast, was the capital of the Chimu kingdom, and at its height it had a population of 30,000. The former capital of the Inca Empire was in Cuzco in Peru. One of the world's most exciting heritage sites is the 15th-century fortress town of Machu Picchu in Peru, which clings to twin mountain peaks in the high Andes Mountains. This is the lost city of the Incas, forgotten by the outside world for hundreds of years.

Across the Pacific Ocean

On the Pacific Islands we find traces of Polynesian and other cultures, including the statues of Easter Island. In Australia most of the heritage sites are natural wonders—rain forests and deserts. But these were also sites of great significance to the Aboriginal peoples who lived there for tens of thousands of years before the arrival of Europeans. Trees, creeks, and boulders for them were like temples or shrines—sacred marks in a landscape. The most famous such site is Uluru, also known as Ayers Rock.

Many of the civilizations featured in this book tried to compete with the wonders of nature by building towers, pyramids, and skyscrapers. The Australian Aborigines were content with the real wonder of the world—the force of nature. As we explore the older sites of world heritage, we find that common inspirations and skills unite humanity. However, we also find a rich variety and diversity of cultures. Every people and region once had its own unique style of architecture. One reason for this was practical. Building materials varied according to the local climate and the availability of raw materials. Modern wonders, by comparison, are generally constructed in a uniform global syle. A modern dam looks impressive, but it appears to be very similar, whether it is in Tajikistan or Brazil. The variety of styles throughout the ages makes the conservation of historical world heritage sites even more important. Our past will inform and influence our present.

▼ Machu Picchu, high up in the Andes Mountains of Peru

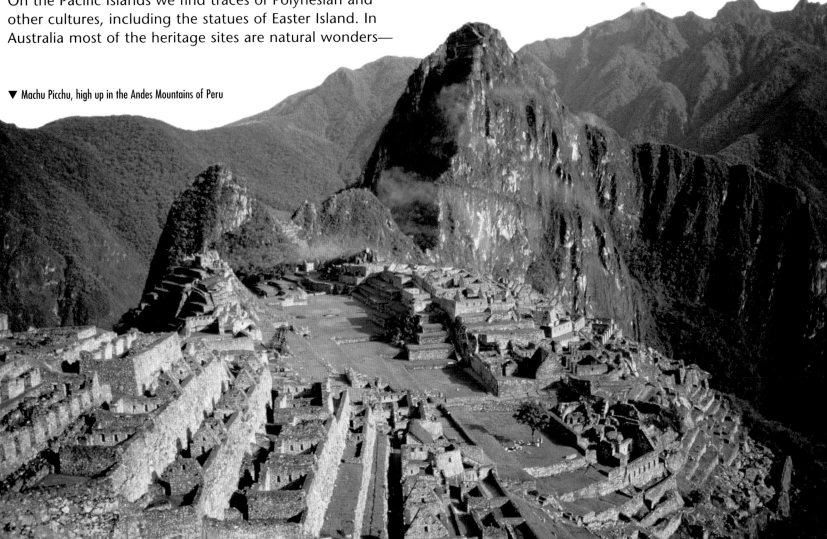

Glossary

amphitheater
A building containing an arena for sports or combat, surrounded by raised seating.

aqueduct
A channel built to carry water, often supported by a bridge.

archaeologist
Someone who investigates and studies ancient ruins and remains.

ball court
The playing area for a sacred ball game that was played by the ancient peoples of Mexico and Central America.

Discus thrower, ancient Greece

beam bridge
A bridge that has a rigid horizontal deck supported by piers.

cable-stayed bridge
A type of beam bridge in which the deck is supported by piers but is also secured by steel cables.

cenote (pronounced sen-aw-teh)
A sunken pool in limestone rock, found in Mexico and Central America.

chacmool
The stone statue of a reclining figure, found in several ancient sites in Mexico and Central America and possibly used during human sacrifices.

clan
A social group that is made up of people who claim descent from a common ancestor.

colossus *plural* **colossi**
Any gigantic statue such as the Colossus of Rhodes.

computer modeling
Using computer calculations to test whether certain options will work, for example, in planning a building.

conservation
Protecting and taking care of an environment or a site.

culture
1 Any way of living, its customs and traditions; **2** Creative activities such as music, art, or literature.

deck
The horizontal section of a bridge, usually supporting a road or a railroad.

flood barrier
A means of protecting coastlines or riverbanks from flooding, often using steel gates that can be raised temporarily.

galley
A large ship that can be propelled by long oars.

gladiator
In ancient Rome someone who was trained to fight in the arena for entertainment.

▲ Carving from Angkor Wat

heritage
Something inherited by a generation from its ancestors such as a fine building or a way of life.

hydroelectric power
Electric power generated from the movement of water.

Industrial Revolution
The rise of new technology and production methods in the 1700s and 1800s.

information technology
Practical methods of storing and retrieving information.

Internet
Electronic communication through a series of computer networks.

irrigation
Methods of bringing water to dry land in order to grow crops.

mausoleum
Any monumental tomb, named after the original Mausoleum of Halicarnassus.

Mesopotamia
The lands around the Tigris and Euphrates rivers, now occupied by Iraq and parts of Syria and Iran.

moai
Huge stone heads that were carved and erected by Polynesians on Easter Island.

mythology
A system of beliefs that attempts to explain creation and the natural world through stories about gods, spirits, demons, heroes, or animals.

nuclear particles
Tiny specks of matter that are found in the nucleus, or core, of an atom.

pharaoh
A ruler of ancient Egypt, thought by the Egyptians to be a god on Earth.

pier
1 A platform that projects into a river or sea; **2** A long pillar that supports a structure such as a bridge.

pile
A strong pole made of timber, concrete, or metal that is driven into rock or a riverbed to support a structure such as a building.

pollution
The poisoning of air, land, or water by waste or chemicals.

pyramid
A monument with a square base and sides that converge to a point on the top.

relief
A carving, usually in stone or clay, that stands out from its background, giving it a three-dimensional appearance.

Renaissance
"Rebirth"—the period of heightened cultural activity that emerged in Europe in the 1400s and 1500s.

solar panel
An array of cells used to generate electricity from the energy of the Sun.

space telescope
A spacecraft with a telescope that is sent into orbit as an observatory.

sphinx
A beast with the body of a lion and the head of human, found in Egyptian mythology. There is a famous sphinx that guards one of the three pyramids in Giza.

steppes
The rolling grasslands of southern Europe and central Asia.

stepped pyramid
A pyramid with layered sections instead of flat sides.

suspension bridge
A bridge with a deck that is supported by suspended cables.

surveyor
Someone who measures the lie of the land before the construction of a road, bridge, or building.

technology
The ways in which science can be applied for practical ends, such as metalworking, mining, or electronics.

temple
A site of religious ritual or worship. The term is used in various religions, including Hinduism, Buddhism, Judaism, and the ancient beliefs of western Asia and Central and South America.

turbine
An engine whose spinning blades are turned by currents of air or water in order to generate power.

tsunami
A gigantic, powerful ocean wave, usually created by an earthquake or an undersea volcanic eruption.

viaduct
Any bridge with unusually high piers, designed to carry a road or railroad.

wind tunnel
A tube in which models of planned buildings or aircraft are tested in a steady current of air, to see how they will react to air currents and stresses.

wonders of the world
Originally, a list of the seven most incredible sights to be seen in the world, as written up by various writers in ancient Greece and medieval Europe.

World Wide Web
A system of linking up information sources across computer networks.

ziggurat
A massive sacred monument found in ancient Mesopotamian cities—a type of stepped pyramid.

▼ The Hubble Space Telescope (HST)

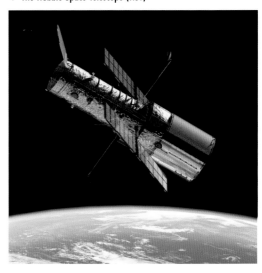

Index

Alexander the Great 20, 22
Alexandria, Egypt 20, 21, 22
Amazons 17
Angkor Thom, Cambodia 28
Angkor Wat, Cambodia 23, 28–29, 38
  and Hindu mythology 29
  and King Jayavarma VII 29
  attack by Tai people 29
  building of 29
  Mouhot, Henri 28
  Mount Meru 29
  Suryavarman II 29
Antipater of Sidon 7, 22
archaeologists 11,17, 22, 28, 30, 31
  marine 21
architects 8, 42, 43
Aztec civilization 32, 38

Babylon 10–11, 14
bridges 39, 46–47
  Akashi-Kaikyo, Japan 47
  beam 46
  Golden Gate Bridge, U.S. 47
  Millau Viaduct, France 46–47
  suspension 46
  Royal Gorge, U.S. 47
  Tower Bridge, England 47
  Tsing Ma Suspension Bridge, China 46
Buddhism 28, 29, 35, 50

Callimachus of Cyrene 7
canals and waterways 36–37, 44
  Grand Canal, China 44
  Panama Canal 44
  Suez Canal 44
  Venice, Italy 36–37
CERN Laboratories, Switzerland 39,
  48-49
  and Internet 49
  and World Wide Web 49
Chichén Itzá, Mexico 23, 32–33, 38
  ball court 32
  ball games 32
  gods of 32, 33
  human sacrifices 32, 33
  ruins 33
  stonework 33

Temple of Warriors 33
  Wall of Skulls 33
  water supplies 33
Christ the Redeemer, Rio de Janeiro,
  Brazil 39, 50–51, 54
Christianity 13, 15, 50
Colosseum (Flavian Amphitheater),
  Rome, Italy 23, 24–25, 38
  building of 24
  engineering of arena 24
  flooding of 24, 25
  games 24, 25
  gladiators 24, 25
  killing of animals 25
Colossus of Rhodes 7, 18–19, 50
  Antigonus I of Cyprus 18
  building of 18
  Chares of Lindos, sculptor 18
  crown 18–19
  Demetrius, invasion by 18
  destruction by earthquakes 18
  Helios, sun god 18
  sale of ruins 18
cyberspace 48, 49

dams 39, 44–45
  and environment 45
  Aswan High, Egypt 45
  engineering of 45
  Glen Canyon, U.S. 39, 44–45
  Grand Coulee Dam, U.S. 45
  Rogun Dam, Tajikistan 45
  Three Gorges Dam, China 45, 54
Djoser, pharaoh 9

Easter Island (Rapa Nui) 23, 30–31, 38
  and Marquesas Islands 30
  and Polynesian people 30
  and slavers 31
  moai (statues) on 30, 31
  tsunami 30
  volcano of Rana Raraku 30, 31
Egypt, ancient 8–9, 20
Egyptians, ancient 7, 8–9
  pharaohs 8, 9
  pyramid builders 9
Eiffel, Gustave 40, 51

Eiffel Tower, France 40, 41, 51

flood defenses 44, 45
  Delta Scheme 45

Genghis Khan 26
gods and goddesses
  Apollo, sun god 15
  Artemis (Diana), goddess of wild
    things 14,15
  Cybele, mother goddess 15
  Hera, wife of Zeus 12
  Helios, sun god 18, 22
  Indra, Hindu god 28
  Nike, goddess of victory 12
  Poseidon, god of the sea 20
  Quetzalcoatl, plumed serpent god 33
  Vishnu, Hindu god 28, 29
  Zeus, king of gods 12–13, 20, 22
Great Pyramid of Khufu 7, 8–9, 22, 43
  and afterlife 9
  building of 8–9
  burial chambers 8, 9
  height of 9
  Khufu, pharaoh 8, 9
  rituals 9
Great Wall of China 23, 26–27, 38
  and Mongols 26, 27
  and Xiongnu 27
  building of 26, 27
  invaders 26, 27
  repair of 27
  watchtowers 27
Greece, ancient 20
Greeks, ancient 7, 9, 10, 11, 22, 23,
  32, 43
  and gods 12, 13, 15, 17, 18–19
  architects 17
  armies 22
  builders 17
  mythology of 12, 17
  poets 22, 54
  sculptors 12, 17
  writers 22
Guggenheim Museum, Spain 39,
  42–43, 54
  architecture of 42

computer modeling 43
Gehry, Frank, designer 42

Hagia Sophia, Constantinople 23
Hanging Gardens of Babylon 7,
    10–11, 22
  Amytis, Queen 10
  Greeks and 11
  irrigation of 11
  Nebuchadnezzar II 10, 11, 22
  planting in 10, 11
Herodotus 7, 22
Hinduism 28, 29, 35
  and god Vishnu 28, 29
Hubble Space Telescope (HST) 39,
    52–53
  imaging 52–53
  mirror 52
  solar panels 52
hydroelectric schemes 44

Inca civilization 32, 38
Internet 49

James Webb Space Telescope (JWST)
    52–53

Khafra, pharaoh 8, 9
Khmer civilization, Cambodia 28, 29
Khufu, pharaoh 7, 8, 22

libraries 39, 48, 49
  Alexandria 48
  Ebla 48
  Library of Congress, Washington,
    D.C., U.S. 39, 49
  Trinity College, Ireland 49

Mausoleum, Halicarnassus 7, 16–17, 22
  Amazons 17
  Artemisia 17
  building of 17
  chariot of gold 17
  destruction by earthquakes 17
  Mausolus, king 16
  statues and friezes 17
Mayan civilization 32, 33, 38
  descendants of 33
Mediterranean Sea 7, 22
Menkaura 9
Mesopotamia 10, 22
Mexico, invasion of 33

Millau Viaduct, France 39, 46–47, 54
  building of 46
  environmental effects 47
  international involvement 47
Ming dynasty, China 27
Moguls 34

Olympic Games 12–13

Persia 10–11
Peru 31, 32
Petronas Twin Towers, Malaysia 39,
    40–41
Pharos of Alexandria 7, 20–21, 22, 40
  and gods 20
  as navigation aid 20, 21
  destruction by earthquake 20
  fuel 21
  maintenance 21
  Ptolemy I 20
  Ptolemy II (Philadelphus) 20
  Sostratus of Cnidus, architect 20
pyramids 8–9, 11, 14, 33
  Chichén Itzá 23, 32–33, 38
  Great Pyramid 7, 8–9, 22, 43
  Saqqara 9

Qin kingdom, China 27
Qin Shi Huangdi, Chinese ruler 27, 58

Rhodes 7, 18, 19, 22
Romans 7, 23, 24–25, 38
  collapse of empire 38
  engineering 38

skyscrapers 39, 40–41, 54
  building of 40–41
  building materials 41
  Burj Dubai Building, U.A.E. (United
    Arab Emirates) 41, 54
  Chrysler Building, U.S. 40
  CN Tower, Canada 41
  elevators in 40
  Empire State Building, U.S. 40, 41
  Rockefeller Center, U.S. 41
  Sears Tower, U.S. 40
  Singer Building, U.S. 41
  Taipei 101, Taiwan 41, 54
space telescopes 39, 52–53, 54
  Hubble Space Telescope (HST)
    52–53
  James Webb Space Telescope (JWST)

52–53
  RATAN 600 52
  Very Large Array (VLA) 52
sphinx, Egypt 8
Statue of Liberty, U.S. 39, 51, 54
  Bartholdi, Frédéric, sculptor 51
  Eiffel, Gustave, engineer 51
  erection of 51
statue of Zeus, Olympia 7, 12–13, 22
  and gods 12
  and Olympic Games 12, 13
  carving of 12
  destruction by fire 13
  Phidias, sculptor 12
Stonehenge, England 23
Sydney Opera House, Australia 39,
    43, 54
  building of 43
  new materials 43
  structure of roof 43
  Utzon, Jørn, architect 43

Taj Mahal, India 23, 34–35, 38
  architecture of 34
  building of 34
  decoration of 34, 35
  expense of building 35
  Mumtaz Mahal 34, 35
  Shah Jahan, emperor 34, 35
Temple of Artemis (Artemisium)
    7, 14–15, 22
  and gods 14, 15
  building of 15
  Herostratus and burning of 15
  rebuilding of 15
  second burning of 15
Toltec civilization 32, 33, 38
tourism 7, 29, 37, 50

Venice, Italy 23, 36–37, 38
  bridges 36
  building of city 36–37
  canals and waterways 36–37
  Doge, the 37
  flooding of 37
  glass making 36
  gondolas 36–37
  islands 36
  trade 36, 37
  vaporetti (water buses) 37

World Wide Web 39

Acknowledgments

The publisher would like to thank the following for permission to reproduce their material.
Every care has been taken to trace copyright holders. However, if there have been unintentional
omissions or failure to trace copyright holders, we apologize and will, if informed, endeavor
to make corrections in any future edition.

Key: *b* = bottom, *c* = center, *l* = left, *r* = right, *t* = top

Cover *l* Photolibrary; Cover *c* Corbis Tim Graham; page *1* Getty Images National Geographic Society; 2–3 Photolibrary JtB Photo Communications; 4–5 Panoramic Images; 8*l* Alamy Werner Otto; 8*r* Corbis Christine Osbourne; 10 Mary Evans Picture Library; 12*cl* Stephane Compoint; 12*b* Stephane Compoint; 13*t* Stephane Compoint; 13*b* Corbis Kin Cheung; 14 Corbis Nik Wheeler; 15 Bridgeman Art Library British Museum, England; 16 Bridgeman Art Library Private Collection; 17 Werner Forman Archive; 18 Bridgeman Art Library Private Collection; 20*tl* Art Archive Dagli Orti; 20*c* Stephane Compoint; 21 Stephane Compoint; 22 Bridgeman Art Library Private Collection; 24–25 Alamy Arco Images; 25*tr* Corbis Tom Brakefield; 26–27 Photolibrary Panorama Media; 26*b* Empics AP; 27*tr* Getty Images Imagebank; 28–29*b* Photolibrary Jon Arnold Images; 28 Heritage Images Partnership; 28–29*t* Corbis Kevin R. Morris; 29*r* Photolibrary Photononstop; 30*l* Corbis Keren Su; 30–31 Getty Images Taxi; 31*t* Corbis Douglas Peebles; 32*bl* Getty Images Stone; 32*c* Art Archive Dagli Orti; 32*tr* Corbis Ludovic Maisant; 33 Getty Images National Geographic Society; 34*tl* Bridgeman Art Library Private Collection; 34*tr* Alamy Steve Allen Travel Photography; 34–35 Impact Photos Yann Arthus-Bertrand; 35*br* Corbis Jim Zuckerman; 36–37 Getty Images Panoramic Images; 36*t* Corbis Jonathan Blair; 37*r* Empics AP; 38 Corbis Keren Su; 40–41 Getty Images Taxi; 41*t* Corbis Bettmann; 42 Photolibrary Index Stock Imagery; 43*t* Photolibrary; 43*b* Corbis Charles & Josette Lenars; 44*tr* Alamy Mike Goldwater; 44*b* Getty Images Hulton; 45 Photolibrary Mary Plage; 46–47 Corbis Reuters; 46*b* Construction Photography; 48*t* Rex Features; 48*b* Photolibrary Dynamics Graphics; 49 Corbis Robert Harding Photo Library; 50–51 Corbis Richard T. Nowitz; 51 Corbis Gail Mooney; 52 NASA/ESA; 52–53 NASA; 53 NASA/ESA; 54 Photolibrary Index Stock Imagery; 55*tl* Corbis Free Agents Ltd; 55*br* Photolibrary Index Stock Imagery; 56*tr* Getty Images Photonica; 56*b* Alamy Rolf Richardson; 57 Getty Images Lonely Planet; 58*tl* Getty Images Imagebank; 58*cr* Photolibrary Jon Arnold Images; 59 Getty Images Taxi; 60*l* Stephane Compoint; 60–61*t* Corbis Kevin R. Morris; 61*r* NASA/ESA; 64 Getty Images Stone